MORE PRAISE FOR
DATING FROM THE INSIDE OUT

"*Dating from the Inside Out* is insightful, focused, personal, and enlightening. Best described, this primer on self-awareness is a starting point in a journey of a lifetime. Through inspirational activities and creative strategies Dr. Sherman skillfully leads the reader into a journey of self-exploration. *Dating from the Inside Out* sends the compelling message you must first be happy and satisfied with who YOU are before You can share your heart."

**—Tara Saltzman, Ph.D., executive dean of
Strategic Initiatives and Global Enterprise for Academic
Development, Nova Southeastern University**

"Dr. Sherman has produced an extremely well written, lucid manual that really goes beyond dating, to living in general. Using her own experiences and those of her clients, she has produced a roadmap that is easy to follow and which, if followed, should lead to a great deal of satisfaction in finding people with whom to be happy. She has translated important concepts from her experience as a therapist and as a dating coach into everyday language that is easy to understand."

**—Dr. Robert Myers, ABPP, psychologist and professor
of psychology at the Institute of Graduate Clinical
Psychology at Widener University**

"Dr. Sherman provides us with refreshing tools and inspiration to embark on a journey that will help us recognize our true life partner and become better acquainted with the partners we choose. She teaches us through guided exercises how to have satisfying dating experiences. Her writing is informed by well-grounded theory and years of success coaching single adults who are dating and in search of happiness."

—Jill Chatanow, speech pathologist

"Used in conjunction with traditional psychotherapy, Dr. Sherman's book provides a useful tool for those ready to embrace a satisfying and lasting relationship. A creative approach to dating that's definitely worth a look."

—Mona Daniels, psychoanalytic psychotherapist

"Dr. Sherman's dating approach takes you into your heart so you can love more fully and attract the mate of your dreams."

—Cindy Ross, a single CFO

DATING
FROM THE
INSIDE
OUT

HOW TO USE THE LAW OF ATTRACTION IN MATTERS OF THE HEART

DR. PAULETTE KOUFFMAN SHERMAN

ATRIA BOOKS
New York London Toronto Sydney

BEYOND  WORDS
PUBLISHING

ATRIA BOOKS

A Division of Simon & Schuster, Inc.
1230 Avenue of the Americas
New York, NY 10020

BEYOND WORDS PUBLISHING

20827 N.W. Cornell Road, Suite 500
Hillsboro, Oregon 97124-9808
503-531-8700 / 503-531-8773 fax
www.beyondword.com

Portions of Portia Nelson's poem "There's a Hole in My Sidewalk" published with permission of Beyond Words Publishing, Inc.

The cases in this book are a composite of clients from Dr. Sherman's practice. Names and situations have been adjusted to protect confidentiality.

Editor: Julie Steigerwaldt
Managing editor: Lindsay S. Brown
Copyeditor: Jennifer Weaver-Neist
Proofreader: Terra Chalberg
Cover/interior design: Sara E. Blum
Composition: William H. Brunson Typography Services

First Atria Books/Beyond Words trade paperback edition February 2008

ATRIA BOOKS and colophon are trademarks of Simon & Schuster, Inc. Beyond Words Publishing, Inc. is a division of Simon & Schuster, Inc.

For more information about special discounts for bulk purchases, please contact Simon & Schuster Special Sales at 1-800-456-6798 or business@simonandschuster.com.

Manufactured in the United States of America

10 9 8 7 6 5 4 3 2 1

Library of Congress Cataloging-in-Publication Data:

Sherman, Paulette Kouffman.
    Dating from the inside out : how to use the law of attraction in matters of the heart / Paulette Kouffman Sherman.
        p. cm.
        1. Mate selection. 2. Dating (Social customs). 3. Man-woman relationships.
    I. Title.
    HQ801.S52442   2008
    646.7'7—dc22
                                                        2007038966

    ISBN-13: 978-1-58270-194-3
    ISBN-10:   1-58270-194-6

The corporate mission of Beyond Words Publishing, Inc.: *Inspire to Integrity*

To my husband, Ian—
my endless love,
inspiration,
and my own last date

CONTENTS

PART 1
UNCONSCIOUS DATING

PART 2
BE THE PARTNER YOU WISH TO ATTRACT

PART 3
CONSCIOUS DATING

❥ · ♥ · ❦

PREFACE

I was thirty-three years old and single when I decided to return to New York from Pennsylvania and date for a year. I had finished my doctoral program, earned my license as a psychologist, and achieved my coaching certification; I felt that it was time for me to choose the man that I would marry. This had long been my dream, but I was finally ready to incubate it. I had been in love and very close to marriage twice, but those partners did not feel completely right. I had many long-term boyfriends but few dating cycles. I knew that I could learn a lot by seeing who was out there and what each person would bring out in me.

So I began my own *Sex and the City* episode (without the sex) and met a lot of people. I landed in an apartment by the beach in Brooklyn and spent mornings journaling and walking the beach. I started to date with the intention of creating romance, love, and partnership as an extension of my deepest self. I reflected on who I was, what I most wanted to create in my life, and who my true life mate would need to be in order to co-create my vision. I married *myself* by choosing to accept who I am and what I created, and committing to honor that in everything I do—including dating.

Then a shift took place. Dating was no longer a goal-oriented, uncomfortable process ripe with rejection. It became an opportunity to share myself, meet others, learn, and have fun. I actually looked forward to dates—whether it was an opportunity to appreciate someone new, learn what I needed in a mate, try a new restaurant, have new experiences, or tour a different neighborhood, I got something out of every date. Dates that did not result in a romantic match were no longer "a waste of my time" because my focus shifted from what was happening "out there" to what was occurring within myself.

I realized that we *attract who we are*. In other words, the clearer I became about myself and what I wanted, the better partner I would attract. The more I liked and accepted myself, the less I participated in game-playing, manipulation, and the superficial aspects and rules of dating that are so widely reinforced. I appreciated my dates for who they were and was authentic, with the knowledge that the right man would stick around.

As I write this, I am now married to the man of my dreams. We are both therapists and have common values, goals, and life visions. We have developed a strong, creative partnership that allows us to be our best selves. It took me a while to get here, but the journey was worth it. I met Ian once I was clear about what I wanted in a partner and had followed some of the principles that I outline in this book. This is why I am delighted to share what I have learned with you so that you, too, can attract the partner of your dreams.

My personal dating journey also affected my professional life. As a psychologist and coach, I began attracting clients who desperately wanted to marry and find a great life mate. They were attractive, smart, professional people who could not understand why none of their relationships had worked. I saw them repeating the same relationship patterns. We looked at how they allowed their old beliefs and relationships to dictate what they were creating in their present dating experience. Once they understood what did not work, we examined what they did want to create so they could date with more awareness, clarity, and effectiveness.

One of my clients, a woman in her early thirties, had always said that she would adopt children but that she would never marry because she was incapable of maintaining a good relationship. After eighteen months of therapy, she allowed herself to date and became engaged to a partner to whom she is now happily married. She was able to shift her old beliefs about what was possible because she recognized her own power and understood how much she had to offer a partner in a relationship. Her new inner vision became so strong that she was able to manifest it in a short period of time.

I began writing a monthly dating column in a magazine where readers write me with their dating questions and issues. I felt intimately connected to their pain. In reality, they were not being rejected by their dates as much as they were rejecting themselves in the process. They were unclear about who they were and what they wanted to create in a relationship. As I pointed out the learning opportunity in each dating dilemma, my readers became excited and started to take responsibility for making their dating experience positive and meaningful.

I also started teaching dating classes and workshops where singles discussed their dating history and beliefs about relationships. They recognized their own story in others' and felt less alone in their dating struggles. Their growing capacity to be authentic and self-accepting translated into more honesty in their relationships. They began attracting better partners, feeling that they deserved them, and were more open to connecting with a life mate.

As a therapist and dating coach, the joy I get from helping people connect with their life partner is incredible. I know how wonderful it is to have a partner who loves, accepts, and supports you, and with whom you can share your life and full self. If more people took the time to learn about themselves and to date with authenticity and clarity there would be less divorce, heartbreak, and broken families. Most of us seek help in finding a job, improving our appearances, losing weight, or learning a new hobby. Why not ask for help for something as important as finding success in our love life? Who you choose as a life mate is one of the biggest decisions you will ever make because it affects everything—your quality of life, emotional state, children, finances, environment, sex life, and just about anything else you can think of. This book will assist you on your journey. You can transform dating from a miserable, confusing process to a fun, enlightening one, and attract the partner of your dreams while learning more about yourself.

By the end of this book, you will know what you were doing before that did not work, who you are now and what you want to create in your love life, the type of partner that fits you best, and how to recognize and attract him. You will also discover what to look for when dating, how to narrow your choices, and when to shift from dating to creating a lasting relationship with the right person. Probably the most wonderful and unexpected gift you will get is that you will fall in love with and marry *yourself* in a much deeper way. In recognizing what is most important to you, you will become committed to manifesting it no matter what happens out there. This is the kind of union that lasts a lifetime.

My best in life and love,

Paulette Kouffman Sherman

Dr. Paulette Kouffman Sherman

ACKNOWLEDGMENTS

My deepest appreciation and thanks to:

My husband, Ian, who constantly teaches me about love, who inspired this project, who read my manuscript, and who rubbed my feet while I was overworked. Thanks for believing in me.

My parents, Miriam and Marc, for raising me and for being stellar examples of passion, hard work, and the belief that life is full of opportunities for creation.

My grandmother Riva, who, as a Holocaust survivor, was a model of courage, love, and how to create life from nothing. Thanks for always being there.

My new family (the Shermans, Gernons, and Lentinis) for welcoming me with love, fun, and support.

The team at Beyond Words Publishing and Atria for their friendly and timely professionalism. To Cynthia Black, who first embraced my book and was the midwife of its launch. Thank you for seeing the potential in a first-time author and for your insight and kindness. To Lindsay Brown, Marie Hix, and Julie Steigerwaldt for their editing and production efforts. To Sara Blum, who designed the beautiful cover. To Lisa Braun Dubbels for her developing

friendship, creative leads, and insight to take my career further. And to Rachel Berry for arranging talks, travel, and publicity on my behalf.

My women angels, Cindy and Aida, for daily chats, support, laughs, and dream-making. To Jill, my kindred spirit; Rachel, Leigh, Karen, and Tan for our very long friendship; Jacki, Todd, Phil, and Brad—my PA gang.

My mentors: Dr. Bruce Lackie for his irreverence, wit, and love of mystery (they are always with me); Dr. Myers for developing my love of being a therapist; Mona Daniels for her ongoing support and wisdom; and Yahosheba and Roger for spiritual inspiration and for sanctifying our union.

Bas, Bill, Tom, Leah, Francine, and all my friends at MNA for their cheer and support.

My clients for always providing me with connection, inspiration, and growth.

And my readers: I thank each of you for being willing to make the love inside of you a reality. Thanks for trusting me on your journey.

INTRODUCTION

How many times have you commiserated with friends after a bad date? Have you ever complained that "all the good ones are taken"? Has a girls' night out ever turned into a man-bashing session? For many people, dating has become a necessary evil, a means to finding The One. It's the dreaded job that gives people more to grumble about than to celebrate. As we engage in this dating gripe fest— in our head or with others—we unwittingly reinforce our dating stereotypes and fears.

This book can change all that. Dating doesn't have to be a frustrating experience, full of rejection and confusion. It can shift to a transformative journey when you learn how to date from the inside out.

I have found that a force known as the Law of Attraction is working in every aspect of our lives. Like gravity or other laws of nature, this principle affects our lives without us really taking notice of it. But by becoming aware of it, we can make it work in our favor. According to this law, we attract what we consistently focus our attention on. As applied to your love life, if you focus on what you don't like about dating or your insecurities, you attract more of the same. If you shift your attention to what you love about yourself and what you would love to attract in a partner, you tend to attract it. To me, The Law of Attraction means that when what you feel, think and do is aligned you most powerfully attract and manifest your desires. So if you are sitting around thinking about how much your ex has hurt you and how all men are cruel, you are unlikely to give your soul mate a chance. In contrast, if you feel great and deserving of a terrific partner you will be open to that opportunity and more likely to draw it.

It is important that you understand what I mean by the Law of Attraction because it is the foundation for part 1 of this book, which will help you remove anything internal that blocks you from realizing your heart's desire. This book will help you start inside yourself, challenging your limiting beliefs and embracing your true self so that you can create the relationship with a partner that you've always wanted.

In the chapters ahead, you'll complete exercises to help you discover how to create better, more successful matches as you examine three major sections:

Part 1: Unconscious Dating will help you under-stand why you keep picking the same type of partner. By identifying your patterns, you can begin to choose with new awareness, freedom, and success.

Part 2: Be the Partner You Wish to Attract—this section shifts your focus to you and what you want to create in your life so you can become the partner you want to attract. You'll choose who you are as a partner, how satisfied you are with your life, and how clear you are about your Relationship Vision. You will discover what you want and then recognize the right partner when you meet them.

Part 3: Conscious Dating will help you date consciously so you can pick a great match. You will discover what you need in a partner, what you won't accept, how to interview partners, and how to create a Dating Action Plan.

This is the perfect time for you to begin a Conscious Dating Journal. Keep a beautiful notebook or journal nearby as you read so you can complete each chapter's exercises. This will be your touchstone. You may also like to refer back to it occasionally to remind yourself of the progress you've made on your dating journey.

FIGURE 1: Conscious Dating Journal

Dating, like anything else in life, is most successful when you are clear, committed, and aligned with your goal. Many popular dating books advise you to change your appearance or to "act differently" to achieve success. This book reminds you that by exploring, embracing, and revealing your true self, you will have the most success in finding the right partner for you. The knowledge and skills you acquire will empower you to make changes the only way possible—through you!

Let's get started!

PART 1

UNCONSCIOUS
DATING

1

YOUR RELATIONSHIP PATTERN: RECREATING OLD EXPERIENCES IN THE PRESENT

Most of us pick the same partner again and again; they just look different! Maybe you thought of attraction as a good thing . . . but you will soon realize that we tend to attract what is familiar, not necessarily what is best for us.

Here's an example: Sheila had an overprotective, demanding, and controlling father. This was her prototype of a relationship with a man. Consciously, she did not want a relationship like this, but it was what she knew. She was astounded to find that she was attracted to a man just like her father. Her new date called her three times a day, became jealous whenever she went out alone, and even had the same first name as her dad! After some time in therapy, Sheila made this dynamic conscious and became better able to create the type of relationship she wanted.

Another client named Melissa asked me, "Why do all the selfish guys pick me?" She asserted that only "bad boys" seemed to like her. She would meet them in a bar, they would sleep together, and these men would never call. As she revealed her story, it was clear that when "nice guys" liked her, she did not find them attractive. Is she a victim of circumstance or is she unconsciously choosing this type of partner in order to transform something?

When something happens to us a few times, it is not accidental. We have to wonder if there is an unconscious pattern at play. There can be many underlying reasons that Melissa continued to pick bad boys. For example, perhaps she was already familiar with dismissive men, like her father. Maybe early on she learned that she was unworthy, so she picked men who treated her that way.

What do I mean by unconscious? It's a word you will hear a lot. Our unconscious mind is where we hold the feelings, thoughts, and memories of which we are not aware. Often we have filed them away because they were too painful. We are equally unaware of how these thoughts and feelings affect our day-to-day experiences. Our job is to make the unconscious conscious so we can make the most of our ongoing experiences in romantic love.

In order to understand the root of your unconscious pattern, you need to really know yourself and examine your past experience. For your first step, identify your unconscious pattern or "the type of mate you continually choose" to create some awareness. This will allow you to shift from being a victim to taking responsibility. You will do this in the next exercise, "Relationship Dissection." When Melissa completed the exercise she could not deny that all the men she was attracted to were selfish . . . and the one constant was that SHE chose them!

Exercise:
Relationship Dissection

In this exercise, you'll look at the type of mate you are attracted to, why you were attracted to them, and what was toxic about the relationship. This helps you to review your past relationships and discover the pattern of partner that you tend to pick again and again.

As I noted in the introduction, you should have a journal to accompany your journey through this book. This will be your Conscious Dating Journal, which will offer a record for visualizing your dating past, present, and future.

Take out your dating journal and make a horizontal list of all your past partners. Write their undesirable qualities in a vertical list beneath each name and then circle the qualities that they all had in common. For example:

Bob	Rick	James	Steve
cheats	cheap	angry	indecisive
Mama's boy	Mama's boy	Mama's boy	Mama's boy

Once you realize that you are picking the same traits again and again, you can assume you have "a type." Your unconscious thoughts attract that type of person because it is familiar. Your unconscious has an antenna that picks whomever is your dating type. In order to recognize the dating hole you fall in, you need to become clear about what your unconscious is seeking. The following poem by Portia Nelson, which I've paraphrased, describes how change works over time.

There's a Hole in My Sidewalk

I walk down a street and there's a big hole. I don't see it and fall into it. It's dark and hopeless and it takes me a long time to find my way out. It's not my fault!

I walk down the same street. There's a big hole and I can see it, but I still fall in. It's dark and hopeless and it takes me a long time to get out. It's still not my fault.

I walk down a street. There's a big hole. I can see it, but I still fall in. It's become a habit. But I keep my eyes open and get out immediately. It is my fault.

I walk down a street. There's a big hole. And I walk around it.

I walk down a different street.

Exercise:
Your Unconscious Want Ad

The best way to be aware of your dating black hole is to place it in black and white, in the form of a want ad. If you are (unconsciously) choosing a partner based on these traits, how does it sound in black and white? Seeing it is bound to wake you up.

Take the circled items from your previous list and create an Unconscious Want Ad. This is the person you attract and are attracted to, not the partner you say you want.

For example:

WANTED:

A man who is uncommitted,
unable to express his feelings,
too close to his mother
and who does not like to spend money.

Often we are unaware of why we pick the people that we do. "It doesn't make sense!" we shout. To our Unconscious Matchmaker it makes perfect sense. You will continue to pick what's familiar until you deal with your past relationships. Melissa, the woman attracted to bad boys, probably experienced being ignored, rejected, and being disposable by a man early on. She never worked through her feelings with her father, so she continues to play it out with similar men. She may have decided early on that all men are this way. She may also have decided that this was how she deserved to be treated.

It seems counterintuitive that what Melissa most wanted—to be cherished—was also what she most feared. But it is not unusual for people to fear the unfamiliar. Melissa was used to being treated badly by men. Although it hurt, it was expected. If Melissa was to open up to a man who treated her well, she might really be disappointed! How could she trust him? These doubts kept Melissa's Unconscious Matchmaker in business by supplying her with the wrong men with whom she felt most comfortable.

Your Unconscious Matchmaker also uses fear to lure you into your same Dating Trap. In this next exercise, you will learn more about the sneaky matchmaking voice operating inside you.

Exercise:
Your Unconscious Matchmaker

Your Unconscious Matchmaker wants you to repeat old patterns until you master them. For example, say your pattern is that you pick cheaters. Your matchmaker says, "You deserve to be cheated on. All men cheat. Don't trust or you will be hurt." Every time the universe brings you another situation with your particular "type" or dating hole, you get an opportunity to make a different choice and walk down a new street. For example, Melissa could now notice when someone was some form of bad boy, and she would not continue to date him once he did not call or left her waiting. Instead she chose men who treated her with respect and were consistent, available and reliable in their affection. She broke her pattern.

To uncover your Unconscious Matchmaker, ask yourself the following questions and record your answers in your dating journal:

- What is your pattern?
- What does your Unconscious Matchmaker say to you about potential partners?
- What does your Unconscious Matchmaker say about you in relation to these partners?
- What would scare you about choosing a partner who was not like this?
- What might an opposite relationship require of you?
- How can you convince your Unconscious Matchmaker that you need to attract a new kind of partner?

Now you have an idea of how you have been programmed to relate to the opposite sex. Programming is hard to change, but the first step is awareness. Once you know your Dating Trap you can begin to create the opposite. The Law of Attraction tells us we should focus on what we want, not what we don't want. So, don't focus on your dating hole. Later we will have you reverse it to create a conscious Want Ad so you will attract what you DO want. Just remember: When you become conscious you have more control over what you create.

YOUR DATING CONTEXT

Another important step to creating what you do want is to notice your Dating Context.

We develop a Dating Context based on past experiences, beliefs, and feelings. Your Dating context is the space you have to create a relationship.

For example, Simone was twenty pounds overweight. She also remembers being teased mercilessly about her weight by a bully in junior high. Men had been interested in her since then, but her old Dating Context was, "All men find me unattractive because I am overweight. Therefore, I cannot date!" During our work together we looked at this more closely, and Simone realized that many overweight women are in relationships and married. She needed to embrace her own worth and beauty, and choose a new Dating Context. Her new perspective stated, "The right partner for me will see my beauty and will love me just as I am." She started dating and has already had some wonderful experiences.

Another client, Jane, was fifty-six years old and widowed. She had been happily married and now felt like there would never be another man for her. It was understandable that she needed to take her time to grieve and to get her bearings. She did this, increasing her support system and adjusting to life without her beloved husband over time. After that, Jane needed to address her Dating Context, which was, "My husband was the only one for me." Jane really wanted a companion in her life going forward. She realized that her husband would have wanted her to be happy, and her new context became, "No one will ever be my husband, but there are many wonderful men out there with whom I can share good times." With this shift, Jane vibrated a different energy and began to attract more fun into her life again.

You can choose a new Dating Context by looking at how your old one no longer serves you. For example, a new Dating Context for bad-boy-attracting Melissa could be, "I used to say that I could only attract disrespectful, unavailable men. Now I am becoming attracted to men who will stay in a relationship with me and who will accept me as I am."

Melissa will need to repeat her new Dating Context regularly. The old one has been reinforced for years, so this new context will need to be practiced. As Melissa continues to integrate her improved mantra, her actions will match her words and close the door to men who do not support her new choice.

Exercise:
Your Old Dating Context
What's your fear about dating? What story about relationships have you told yourself and maybe even your friends?

People have many dating fears. They think they'll continue to get rejected, will invest in someone only to be lied to or cheated on, will be deceived about who someone really is, and so on. These things can happen in life and in dating. However, there are also many times that they don't happen! If this is the lens through which you view all your past and future dating experiences, then you are vibrating fear and not allowing in all the wonderful romantic possibilities. It's time to create a reality-based, positive context that will serve you instead of sabotage you.

This shift in context can take many shapes; here's an example: Shana tried to learn about her old Dating Context, where it came from, and how to apply a productive new one. Her father had an affair, and she was then afraid that all men would leave her. She had to work through these steps:

Shana's Dating Context

Event/Fear: *My father had an affair; so men will hurt and leave me.*

Old Dating Context: *Dating stinks. I have to risk rejection only to find a man who will probably leave me in the end anyway.*

New Dating Context: *Not all men leave. I have the opportunity to experience different people and to choose who I want to spend time with. I can learn about myself, have fun, try new things, and learn from every person I meet. I can create lasting love.*

Now it's your turn. Take out your dating journal and recall a painful event that may have caused you to create the old Dating Context that is not serving you. Think about the story that you continuously tell yourself about dating and relationships and then write your new Dating Context in your journal. Let this new perspective be your mantra, and don't give that old context room to slip back into your thoughts.

Now that we have unearthed your limiting beliefs and Dating Context, we will examine your past relationship baggage in the next chapter. When you understand and clear old pain, it becomes possible to have many different kinds of relationships. Only then can you really see the person before you with new eyes.

2

UNPACK YOUR DATING BAGGAGE: LEAVING YOUR PAST BEHIND YOU

We have all had painful experiences that we carry with us. Unless we recognize their impact and put them in the past, we will carry them from one relationship to the next. For example, Ana's dad was married for eighteen years when he cheated on her mother. He had always been Ana's hero. Then he lied to her and she was devastated. She was hurt about his behavior, but she was also mad at herself for being so naïve about who he was. The event was twice as devastating, making her distrust herself as well as men.

The baggage that Ana began to carry contained a number of unresolved feelings and negative impressions:

"You are a bad judge of character."
"Men are not what they seem."
"Don't trust men."
"Men will cheat and break your heart."

Can you imagine Ana or anyone else suppressing this baggage on a date? "Hi, nice to meet you. I'd reach out to you, but I have this huge bag to contend with . . ."

Another client, Marissa, was sixty-six years old, divorced, attractive, and intelligent. She had been married for twenty-one years and single for the same amount of time. She liked her life, friends, and activities but felt lonely and wanted a companion. Though she was a disciplined action-taker, she had done very little in the way of dating. When I asked her why, she said, "Men my age just want young chickies. I am not attracted to much older men and the available ones who are my age are not usually good enough for me." She had it all figured out, shutting the door to finding love before she even began! She probably had some evidence that men like younger women, and a few experiences that suggested the available men her age did not meet her standards. Instead of casting her net wide and letting in experiences that would challenge her beliefs, Marissa let these past experiences hold her back.

Past hurt, rejection, and disappointment color how you step into your new relationships. You can make a fresh start by becoming more aware of the old fears that stop you from loving today.

Exercise:
What Baggage Do You Bring on Your Date?

To stop the limiting beliefs of old relationships from getting in the way of your next dating experience, you must first identify those beliefs. To do this, draw some large suitcases in your dating journal and then fill them with the negative beliefs, experiences, and feelings you carry around from past relationships.

Some examples that I see in my counseling practice include clients who say, "men don't want marriage" or "men won't like me because I am a powerful, successful woman." Once a client looks at the facts and not just the story they've made up, things begin to shift. The client who feared that no man wants marriage began to acknowledge that many men are married. In fact, many men come to me for coaching and classes because they want to attract a life mate and relationship. This is a fact that women in the same classroom refuse to acknowledge because of their past baggage. These women miss out on what is right before them! My other client, who feared men would not like her due to her success, could see over time that the right man would really admire a powerful, successful woman. Both these clients were coming from a place of pain, scarcity, and "don't want" when I first began working with them. Once they could release the old baggage, they had room to affirm a different possibility. The "successful" client could then say to herself, "The right man will admire and adore my skills and talents." My other single client began to believe, "Many men marry, and the right partner for me will never let me go." These statements galvanized the positive energy that they now direct towards themselves and their future.

Now go back to your dating journal. With the contents of your baggage displayed before you, identify the origin of each old belief and record it in your journal. Really look at how that particular experience, person, or thing has made an impact on you and recognize how much space and negative energy you have devoted to these burdens.

You can't change your past experiences. Both good and challenging things happen in life. It is your job to try and learn something from what happened and release what no longer serves you. Your pain is real and you can't deny it. Feel it and let it move through you so you don't carry it into your future in a dysfunctional way.

Look at the facts of your traumatic experience. For example, in Ana's case her father had an affair. The story she made up around that was that she was naïve and had bad judgment, and that all men were untrustworthy. Does that necessarily follow from the fact that her dad had an affair? He had problems with Ana's mother, which had nothing to do with Ana. Ana internalized this in an emotional, train-wreck moment, and it now colors all her relationships with men.

According to the Law of Attraction, the more you hang on to your past pain and story, the more pain you will continue to attract. By releasing the old beliefs that no longer serve you, you minimize the possibility of repeating those past experiences in your life. This creates room for the new kind of relationship you most want to attract.

Let's look inside your baggage to see what you are carrying around and how you can release it. Now that you have identified your limiting beliefs, lets challenge them.

Exercise:
Unpack Your Bags
In this exercise you'll look at your beliefs and challenge them so you can travel light. For example:

Belief: ⟶ **Challenge:**

Men will leave me. Not all men leave. Plenty of men are in lasting marriages. I am able to create a lasting, trusting relationship.

Now you do it. In your dating journal draw your suitcase and write your baggage beliefs inside. Draw an arrow to symbolize your changing viewpoint, and write a challenging belief. From here on, I want you to repeat that challenge on a regular basis.

BE COMPLETE WITH YOUR PAST LOVES

Another important component of being truly present in a new relationship is being complete with old flames. This means you need to come to terms with all the regret, disappointment, or longing you hold from past relationships and partners. You will know you are complete when you could bump into them again someday and not feel angry or uncomfortable.

The next exercise will help you to complete your old relationships. It is an activity that you can do internally, but it can be even more powerful if you make direct contact. If you choose to contact an ex-boyfriend, first be clear about what you want to say. This can be positive or negative. Perhaps you never got to say how sad you felt when he cheated on you, or conversely, you never got to tell him how much you loved him and enjoyed your time together, even though it did not work out. Whatever you are holding onto, it's time to complete it. Ask the other person just to listen for five minutes and let you get your thoughts out. This is not a dialogue, and it does not require a reaction from him. You could tell him that if he has something to say to feel complete, you will listen to him. This is not about maintaining that relationship or achieving anything for the future. You are just completing your past. You may be having qualms as you're reading this and thinking, "That's crazy! My ex-boyfriend will think I am still hung up on him after five years if I call him now!" I had the same fear when I dialed my ex years ago. Then I realized that I was doing this for myself and his reaction was his choice. I did not need a response from him. I wanted to be fully self-expressed and to release any past emotion. Besides, what is crazier, making a call to someone from your past or letting your past direct your future? Achieving completion not only frees you but it also allows past partners to be released from that energy and to move on as well.

Exercise:
Extinguish Your Old Flame
This exercise focuses on the process of letting go so that you can date without bringing the old faces from the past with you.

Begin by making a list of all your past relationships and then list anything you are holding onto as a disappointment or regret, including anything you wish you or your former partner had done differently.

Next, while looking at your list, answer the following questions for each relationship. Hold that person's face in your mind, and record your answers in your journal.

- What are you willing to let go of?
- What are you willing to be responsible for?
- What are you willing to forgive?
- What is now possible due to letting go?

TAKE THE WISDOM, LEAVE THE REST

With every failed relationship comes knowledge. Even in the worst situations, there is always something to learn (for example, maybe you learn to avoid dating married men or to talk about what you both want in a relationship sooner). Rather than looking at past relationships as examples of your relationship incompetence, look at them as a huge melting pot of wisdom that you now have at your disposal.

Before you completely say good-bye to your past flames, take some time to hang on to the wisdom you have gleaned from the experiences. Close your eyes and see yourself climbing the stairs, one relationship step at a time, in order to meet your ideal partner. With every step, look closely at what you have learned. Try to get past any lingering negative feelings, and distill from the experience the kernel of knowledge. Ask yourself how that knowledge will benefit you going forward. Do this for every relationship.

When you are finished, savor your newly found state as a "wise dater."

ADDRESS YOUR UNDERLYING FEELINGS

After you let go of your past baggage, revise your old Dating Context, and find completion with your past relationships, you can begin to look at the feelings that were underneath the pain in your heart.

Sherry was fifty-six years old and divorced. Her husband had left her for his secretary, and she had been shocked and lonely ever since. Before Sherry married, she believed in love, fidelity, trust, romance, and longevity. Her divorce and her husband's choices were understandably painful, but they also caused Sherry to alter her beliefs about love.

The divorce was a dramatic chapter but not Sherry's whole love story. Sherry had many other early experiences of love, and she could continue to have new experiences with partners who would make different choices than her husband. Once Sherry understood this and she released her husband emotionally, she was able to vibrate her own feelings of love, trust, and faith again, attracting positive prospects into her life.

It's painful when relationships end. No matter what the reason for the break-up, they tend to make people build a wall around their hearts. Feelings of anger, hurt, sadness, and helplessness keep you stuck. Scientists once did an experiment where they would wave cheese above rats in a plastic cage. The rats would jump but could not reach the cheese, due to the lid. Eventually the rats became so frustrated that they stopped jumping when the cheese was presented. Even when the lid was removed, the rats would not jump to get the cheese. This phenomenon is called "learned helplessness." When you let past disappointments keep you stuck, you become like those rats, in a cage of your own making. Don't let frustrations from past experiences prevent you from jumping for what you want in the future. Before you had any bad dating experiences, you believed in love and knew what it felt like to freely give and receive love and trust. This is your natural state. The following exercise will help reconnect you with your original feelings about love so that you can share yourself openly in relationships.

Exercise:
What Is Really in Your Heart?

In this exercise you will get in touch with how you felt about relationships before you were last hurt. This will remind you that your last experience was just one chapter of your love story, not the entirety. Behind all the pain, your true self is waiting to emerge.

Draw a big heart in your dating journal, big enough to fill the entire page. Fill in the heart with your original feelings of love—the ones that were covered over. Reflect on these feelings and experience them like they were new. Forget why you abandoned those original beliefs and instead focus on recapturing that feeling of newness, optimism, and hope. The past is behind you; remind yourself of what was in your heart before you were ever hurt so you can vibrate that energy again. Reclaim the power of love in your natural state.

Another critical unconscious pattern that can limit your romantic relationship is your early relationship with your opposite sex parent and your parents' relationship with each other. In the next chapter, we will revisit how these factors have shaped your romantic choices and expectations.

3

Discover Your Original Blueprint: Making Your First Relationships Conscious

Often our early relationships color all future ones. The dynamic between you and your father, and your father and your mother, play a critical role in how you behave in relationships. For example, Alice's parents had a marriage rife with power struggles. Her mom constantly nagged and complained, and her passive dad eventually acquiesced to his wife with resentment. As a young woman who was dating, Alice tended to recreate this dynamic with her boyfriends. Things started out wonderfully and then she would find ways to improve and control her boyfriends, like her mom did with her dad. This pattern bewildered Alice because she consciously knew that this was not something she wanted to recreate. It just seemed to happen when she wasn't looking.

Relationship dynamics like this leave an impression on us as we pass through childhood and begin to create our own relationships. We are all growing and tending our own Relationship Tree. We may not have planted it or created our early growth experiences, but we choose how we will grow from it. What new life (thoughts, feelings, experiences, and beliefs) will arise going forward?

The next exercise will help you to create a vision for your Relationship Tree and determine how you will facilitate its growth going forward. Look at the sample tree in the exercise. How can you make peace with each of its parts so that it can continue to grow and reach out?

 ### Exercise:
Your Relationship Tree
In your dating journal draw a large tree with space to fill in the different branches. Extend a line from each branch and then fill out your tree with the following sections: the roots of the tree are the originating event, the tree holes are the wounds, the branches are the results in your life, the leaves are the positive aspects you were not seeing, and the new growth is the belief you need to adopt in order to grow from it. Here's an example:

Now let's look specifically at your relationship with your father and how it impacts your current view of relationships.

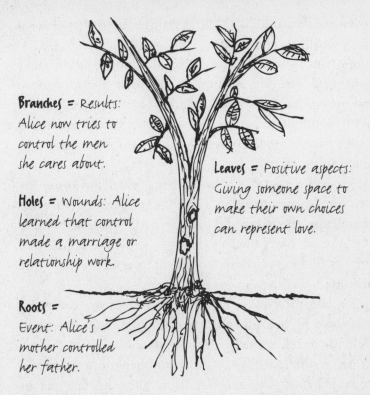

Branches = Results: Alice now tries to control the men she cares about.

Holes = Wounds: Alice learned that control made a marriage or relationship work.

Leaves = Positive aspects: Giving someone space to make their own choices can represent love.

Roots = Event: Alice's mother controlled her father.

New Growth = Necessary action: Alice would need to give her mate space to make decisions and express himself, and to see what new beauty results in her relationships. Her new affirmation could be, "I allow my mate freedom to live his own life peacefully and respectfully."

FIGURE 2: Relationship Tree

DECONSTRUCTING DAD

Your relationship with your father was your first love with a man, and as such it has a profound impact on your relationships with all the other men you enter a relationship with, whether you realize it or not. It is important to uncover those early emotions and the story you made up about him. Doing this allows you to release painful feelings and create something totally new, with a different person. By completing the past, you make room for a conscious adult relationship with a man, in the present.

Jen had a controlling father who yelled and made her cry. She learned never to speak up or disagree. Once she was dating, she never told her boyfriend what she needed. As a result of bottled-up feelings, she developed panic attacks. She expected her boyfriend to react the same way that her father did.

Jen began to understand that as a child she was over-whelmed by her father's rage, but as an adult, she could defend herself. Slowly, this realization allowed her to create a different type of relationship with a man. She took baby steps to tell her dates how she felt and to express her differences, and saw that nothing terrible happened. Over time, she was fully able to express her feelings and needs with her dates. This resulted in more authentic, healthy relationships. Your relationship with your father determines your relationship style with men. Let's examine this in the next exercise.

Exercise:
Your Relationship with Your Father
In your dating journal, write down your answers to the following questions about your relation-ship with your father.

- What was good in your relationship with him during childhood?
- What was challenging about it?
- What did you need that you did not get?
- What do you still hold against your father?
- Do you accept your father for who he is and who he is not?
- Can you appreciate him for what you did get?
- Are you willing to do that now?
- How would this emotional shift serve you in future relationships?
- What would it take for you to do this now?

Often clients have a good relationship with their father and want to marry a man "just like dear old Dad." This is understandable and often results in a healthy relationship, but it's important to be sure that this is an adult choice and not a way of remaining a child, by keeping Dad around in some way. Since our unconscious programming is strong, we tend to replicate the familiar to some extent. If you can have a positive, accepting relationship with your father, you are more likely to have one with a similar husband. If you had a difficult relationship with your father, it is important to be conscious so you do not pick similar men or create a similar relationship dynamic going forward. If you need more help with this process, seek out a qualified therapist to help you gain more clarity about your particular patterns. Whether your relationship with your father was healthy or contentious, it will serve you in future relationships if you are conscious of it and aware of how it affects your current life.

The Parental Dynamic

The first blueprint of how a relationship looks derives from your parental relationship. It is important to understand that relationship so that you do not recreate it. Even if your parents had the perfect marriage, part of being an adult is to consciously choose your own vision of what you will create. Your vision could be equally wonderful, but it may look different than that of your parents.

For example, Susan's parents had a nontraditional marriage. Her mother bossed around her father and was the breadwinnermaking. Now Susan is in a relationship with a man who makes no money and is living in her house rent-free. Susan is angry about it, and constantly demeans him. She knew this man would be reliant on her, so why did she pick him? Until she understands her parental relationship, Susan cannot be spontaneous in her current ones. To have free choice, she must recognize the old model she is renacting.

Our default position is the familiar. For Susan to choose an independent, secure man, she would have to develop a whole new way of being in her relationships. It may even feel like she is not in control. Although Susan says that she wants this, on an emotional level it might feel uncomfortable for her. She needs to come to terms with this conflict in order to create a new type of relationship.

Exercise:
Understanding Your Parental Model of Relationships

You are likely to recreate your parental relationship unless you become conscious of it and choose a different dynamic. In order to become more aware of your parental model, ask yourself the following questions in your dating journal:

- What was good about your parents' relationship?
- What was destructive in their relationship?
- How do you express those characteristics in your relationships now?
- What would you like to do differently?
- How will you accomplish that?
- What gets in your way?
- How will you begin to overcome this obstacle?

Most of us learn what it means to be in a romantic relationship by watching our parents. This parental blueprint has a strong emotional pull, unless we make it conscious; only then can we freely choose to create something different. Be clear about how you want to behave in your relationship and the new dynamic you wish to create.

So much of what we do in dating is unconscious, fear-based, and from the past, causing us to fall into the same Dating Traps. Next, we will discover how most of us learn a defensive style in our relationships to avoid getting hurt. We will identify your Defensive Dating Style and learn how to move beyond it, so you can be more open as a date/partner in the future.

4

Your Defensive Dating Style: Erecting Walls That Define Your Dating Style

Let's face it: dating can be scary. You meet a total stranger, let him get to know you, and see if he will squash your heart. Especially if you have been through this a few painful times, you have probably developed a few tricks along the way to protect yourself. I am not talking about getting a private detective or stalking your date. I am talking about a Defensive Dating Style of which you may not even be aware. Do you have a friend who dates man after man and never lets any of them in? They all fall in love with her, but she seems to care for none of them?

According to my typology, this would be The Independent. She has learned not to let herself become emotionally involved, for fear of being hurt. As you read this chapter, you will learn about fifteen Defensive Dating Styles and can see which one you fit.

For example, if you are The Romantic you may often find that you "fall in love with love." You display dramatic feelings and gestures for partners without really knowing them. This dating style prevents you from truly loving and knowing the other person fully and prevents your partner from knowing the real you over time.

Each dating style is an attempt to create safety in relationships. For example, Samantha was The Needy dater. She decided that in order to be loved and in a committed relationship, she had to do everything with her partner. She equated need with love. Her mother had this type of co-dependent relationship with Samantha and with her husband. Over time Samantha recognized her Defensive Dating Style, and had to devise a new definition of love. She later defined love as two independent people who also loved each other, allowing her to attract that kind of mate and relationship.

Kim was a Player. When she was young, she learned to never show her feelings and to keep things light. Her family moved around, and she learned to get attention by being the life of the party. This allowed her to meet people quickly without letting them get to know her. In this way, Kim protected herself from getting too close and being hurt. This pattern affected her relationships with men.

In the next exercise, you will take the quiz to discover your Defensive Dating Style. From there we'll explore how your style hinders you and what you can do about it. Knowing your particular dating tendencies allows you to become more aware of your dating psychology and its particular limitations so you can begin to make new choices.

Exercise:
What's Your Dating Style?

Take a guess about your Defensive Dating Style from the list below and then take the corresponding quiz to find out for sure.

- The Aristocrat
- The Avoider
- The Control Freak
- The Impulsive
- The Independent
- The Needy
- The Partier
- The Passive-Aggressor
- The Perfectionist
- The Pleaser
- The Project Master
- The Romantic
- The Scrooge
- The Serial Monogamist
- The Player

Your Defensive Dating Style Quiz

In your dating journal, write down how many times you answer yes to the questions beneath each style. If you answer yes three or more times, this is your Defensive

Dating Style. Read the whole quiz because you may have more than one style, which means that you have a combination of ways that protect you in your relationships.

THE ARISTOCRAT
1. Do you expect people to always follow your agenda?
2. Do you expect to be catered to at all times?
3. Are you often dissatisfied with the amount of effort expended on you?
4. Do you expect to be worshipped while remaining aloof towards your dates?
5. Are you often told that you are "high maintenance"?

THE AVOIDER
1. Do you procrastinate?
2. Do you avoid things that scare you?
3. Do you say you are going to do something but your actions don't match your words?
4. Do you miss opportunities by over-analyzing?
5. Do people describe you as someone who is afraid to make choices?

THE CONTROL FREAK
1. Do you like to be in control of your relationship?
2. Do you like to make all the choices and decisions?
3. Do you apply pressure so the other person conforms to your expectations?
4. Do people tell you that you need to be in charge?
5. Do dates say they cannot compete with you and your standards?

THE IMPULSIVE

1. Are you always being told to take more time with decisions?
2. Do you move on before taking the time to get to know someone?
3. Do you take a lot of risks without using your head?
4. Do you assume rather than experience?
5. Do you avoid relationships that seem predictable?

THE INDEPENDENT

1. Are you living by intellect more than by your feelings?
2. Do you dislike being vulnerable?
3. Do people feel you don't care much on your dates?
4. Do you find it challenging to express your feelings?
5. Do people describe you as cold or stuck up?

THE NEEDY

1. Do you expect all your dates to be there whenever you call?
2. Do you feel your date has to fix you or your life?
3. Do you often ask your dates for help or guidance?
4. Do you appear like you can't get through life alone?
5. Do you require a lot of care and attention to be trully happy in life?

THE PARTIER

1. Do you only stay in relationships that are fun?
2. Do you run at the first sign of attachment or problems?
3. Do you avoid pain in your life?
4. Do you have trouble being serious?
5. Do people tell you it is time to grow up?

THE PASSIVE-AGGRESSOR

1. Is it hard to confront your dates when you are upset?
2. Do dates tell you that you seem angry, even when you don't realize it?
3. Do you create problems in order to distance yourself?
4. Do you have a hard time discussing what makes you upset and angry?
5. Do people ever tell you that you hurt them in indirect ways?

THE PERFECTIONIST

1. Do you usually find something wrong with your dates?
2. Do you focus on faults more than good points?
3. Does everyone you meet seem "not good enough"?
4. Do you spend a lot of time in regret?
5. Do you think you will find the perfect mate?

THE PLEASER

1. Do you focus on whether a person likes you instead of the reverse?
2. Do you usually adjust yourself to meet your partner's desires above your own?
3. Are you unlikely to assert your needs in a relationship?
4. Do you feel you have to be "your best" to be liked?
5. Do people tell you that you should say what you want more?

THE PROJECT MASTER

1. Are most of your partners "projects" to save?
2. Do you spend a lot of time improving your partner's situation?

3. Does being a caretaker make you feel like a hero?
4. Do people always tell you that you date losers?
5. Have any of your dates ever been happy, self-sufficient people?

THE ROMANTIC

1. Do you romance whomever you meet?
2. Are you thinking about marriage after the first date?
3. Do you put your date on a pedestal before you've gotten to know each other?
4. Do people say that you are more in love with love than with your partner?
5. Do you scare away your partner with grand gestures?

THE SCROOGE

1. Do you think every relationship will fail?
2. Do people always describe you as negative?
3. Do you think about being hurt more than you think about being happy?
4. Do you feel your romantic life is earmarked for disaster?
5. Are you afraid to try in dating?

THE SERIAL MONOGAMIST

1. Are you always in a long-term relationship?
2. Do people always ask you what you see in your partner?
3. Do you avoid being single and hate being alone?
4. Do you avoid dating a number of people at once?
5. Is being in a relationship more important than the partner that you choose?

THE PLAYER

1. Do you go from one partner to the next?
2. Do you ever get a rush from the number of conquests you have?
3. Do people tell you that you have commitment issues?
4. Do people view you as shallow and escapist?
5. Do you feel more powerful in pursuit of a relationship than in one?

WHAT YOU CAN DO ABOUT YOUR DATING STYLE

Now that you've found your Defensive Dating Style(s), it's time to notice how, when, and why you adopt this role. Keep in mind that the causes I've suggested are only possibilities; they vary according to each person and situation. This will give you a range of styles within which you can recognize your tendencies to protect yourself from being hurt in love. Read on to learn more about your dating style and how you can improve upon it.

THE ARISTOCRAT:
It's all about me.

Hilda was used to getting everything her way. She was "daddy's little girl" and expected similar treatment from her dates. Men often found her confidence intriguing at first, but they later felt the relationship should be more reciprocal.

It is good to know who you are and what you want, but a relationship is about *both* people. A healthy relationship requires understanding your partners needs as well as your own.

Possible Cause:
Perhaps you grew up being catered to and given everything you wanted. You weren't expected to consider how your actions affected others because the focus was always on you.

Action:
Stop to ask yourself what you give back in your relationships. Consider compromising your desires sometimes in the spirit of mutuality and discover the benefits of a reciprocal relationship.

THE AVOIDER:
Why do today what I can do tomorrow?

Rebecca talked about dating and marriage. She was in her early forties and wanted to have children, but she never seemed to make it to the singles events she put on her calendar. She subscribed to many online dating sites, but she rarely wrote to any dating prospects. When Rebecca was scared, her actions and her words did not match. She retreated.

Opportunities are plentiful, but fear can stop us from making choices that serve us *now*. Don't let the love of your life pass you by because you are too busy avoiding responsibility. Take action today.

Possible Cause:

Often procrastination runs in the family. Did your parents put things off when they were worried about something? This approach hinders progress and misses any immediate opportunities that would have been available had things been addressed immediately.

Action:

Don't let fear stop you from seizing opportunities. Take baby steps toward realistic dating goals, and celebrate every victory. Don't wait for love to find you.

THE CONTROL FREAK:
I must be in control.

Lauren loved finding men whom she could mold. She would scream, whine, point, and lecture until they did things her way. Eventually, either she would lose respect for them or they would leave her because she did not respect their choices.

It is good to shape your own destiny, but you must also allow people to make their own choices. Don't let your need to control destroy the mutuality and surprise in your relationships.

Possible Cause:

Maybe your parent made all the choices so now you are asserting your power in your adult relationships. Or maybe one or both of your parents were very loose in their guidance, forcing you to take control at an early age. It feels scary to allow your partner to decide things for the both of you sometimes.

Action:

Notice your fear, take a deep breath, and let your partner make more choices. Loosen your grip and see what happens. Then examine what you learn from this experience in mutually.

THE IMPULSIVE:
I don't look before I leap.

Amy constantly met men in bars thinking they were The One. She slept with them right away and then felt disappointed about who they turned out to be.

Taking risks in relationships is a good thing, but it is also important to think things through before making big decisions. You are someone who goes on your impulses and whims. You leap into a relationship before you even know what you are getting. It may benefit you to know someone over time before making that commitment. Slow down.

Possible Cause:

Maybe you identify with an impulsive person in your family. This person didn't think about the costs of making quick decisions or about how it could benefit him or her— and others in the family—to think before acting.

Action:

Take your time, ask friends for their perspective, and examine pros and cons of your choices while dating. Wait at least four months before becoming exclusive.

THE INDEPENDENT:
I appear cold and self-centered.

Lisa was cool and fun. She never appeared emotionally involved with her dates, giving the impression that she was independent and could take them or leave them. Men liked her style at first because there was no pressure and she seemed centered and self-assured. But over time, most men got frustrated and lost interest because they never felt important enough. They did not want to keep investing in a relationship with her.

It is great to be independent, but your date wants to feel appreciated. He wants to know that you care for him and value him. Sometimes this gets lost in your indifferent communication.

Possible Cause:

Perhaps pride was a big thing in your family. Maybe it was not OK for you to show vulnerability by expressing your true feelings.

Action:

Practice being vulnerable by expressing feelings and appreciation; be real in your relationships. Then identify what you lose when you let go of your pride and compare it to what you can gain.

THE NEEDY:
I need help to get through life.

Joni came from a very close family and spoke to her mom three times a day, even though she lived in a different city. When she dated, she expected her date to show his love by anticipating her every need. This is what she was used to in her relationship with her mother, but it was not appropriate on a date. Her expectations were unrealistic: she wanted her dates to read her mind and was disappointed when they inevitably failed.

It is good to ask for help, but it is also important to stand on your own two feet. Healthy relationships consist of two strong people who take care of themselves and give to each other.

Possible Cause:

Maybe in your family you were given the message that it was bad to be independent. Or maybe you did not have a relationship model where both partners could meet their own needs and still be together.

Action:

Learn to fulfill your own needs more by practicing the taking and giving of space. Then identify your fear of being left alone, and work to overcome it with small, independent steps. The next time that you want to ask someone what to do, resist the temptation. Review your options and make your own choice. This requires practice but you can do it!

THE PARTIER:
My relationships must be fun!

Herman worked and partied hard. Every time he dated and got into a relationship, he balked at the first sign of a challenge. He believed that relationships should always be fun. As soon as he was required to talk about something or to compromise with a girlfriend, he was out the door. His mate would feel unimportant, and he would be off to the next fun time.

It is great when life (and dating) is fun, but most of us know that it also involves work. No relationship or person is perfect; challenges are part of the package. Unless you recognize this, you may never participate in a meaningful, mature, long-term relationship.

Possible Cause:

Perhaps you had a parent who put pleasure before commitment, taking energy away from you and others who depended on him or her. An environment based on whimsy was far from the security you needed to feel safe as you grew up. But you adapted, choosing to keep things fun and not to depend on others too much.

Action:

Notice your fear when a relationship suddenly requires something from you emotionally. Instead of running, try to face the issue and work it through. What happens to you when you take a relationship seriously—are you afraid and uncomfortable? Do you run when it becomes boring? Journal about what happens when you settle down with one person and need to do the work of a truly committed relationship.

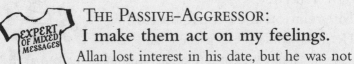

THE PASSIVE-AGGRESSOR:
I make them act on my feelings.

Allan lost interest in his date, but he was not comfortable telling her. He kept standing her

44

up and forgetting to call her until she got so mad that she broke up with him. He got the end result he wanted in a roundabout way and never had to be direct about it.

If you are someone who does not directly express your feelings, this could destroy your relationships. We all know people who push our buttons instead of just stating what makes them angry.

Possible Cause:

Perhaps anger was not safe in your family and you could not choose how to express your true feelings.

Action:

Identify and express your anger directly; communicate your feelings so you and your partner can discuss them. By practicing safe ways to admit what you are feeling in relationships, you can see that nothing bad happens and will begin to change your past patterns.

THE PERFECTIONIST:
No one is good enough for me.

Kelly was an athlete and an honors student, and she had an impressive job and contacts. No matter whom she dated, she found them sub-par. Like Jerry Seinfeld's character on television, she found that the littlest things were red flags. This style eliminated the opportunity to get to know many wonderful people.

Often perfectionists are waiting for something better so they don't appreciate what they DO have now. It is great to better yourself, but if perfectionism is your roadblock to love, you could be passing up a lot of great people to attain a fantasy.

Possible Cause:

Perhaps this was the way your parents treated you. It was not enough for you to have strengths and weaknesses. They constantly berated your handicaps, without equally praising your strengths, and now you have learned to speak to yourself and others this way.

Action:

Focus on the positive. Consider that everyone has strengths and weaknesses. If you usually look for the other person's problems, begin to look for his strengths. Ask yourself if you are being reasonable about your expectations of others and yourself. Give dates more of a chance.

THE PLEASER:
It's all about them.

Hope always tried to be the perfect person for her dates. She never asserted her own needs, so her dates did not really know who she was.

It's good to think about the person you're dating but not to the exclusion of yourself. It is important to know who you are and what you want in a relationship. If you only worry about whether your partner likes you, one day you may wake up and realize that your partner does not really know you, that you don't really like your partner or the person you've become.

Possible Cause:

Think about how you became a pleaser in the context of your family. Were you always expected to please others first, while your own needs came second or last? Because nobody seemed to care about your desires, you quit caring too.

Action:

Examine whether your choice to please is a "should" or a "want to." What has been the cost and/or benefit of this choice? Give more thought to what you want in your relationships and the ways in which you can let people know what you want.

THE PROJECT MASTER:
I find "projects" to save.

Sonya loved dating men who needed her in some way. She saw their potential and wanted to bring it out and save them from themselves. She devoted time to their growth instead of her own, and often they ended up resenting her for trying to change them.

You love to help people and you feel best being a savior. The problem is that most people change only when they want to, and the hard work must come from them! Ask yourself why you don't just pick someone whose life is *already* the way they (and you) want it to be?

Possible Cause:

Perhaps your role in the family was "savior," with everyone coming to you with their problems. Though there was likely a lot of unwelcome responsibility placed on your shoulders with this role, it also generated a feeling of importance and purpose.

Action:
Notice if you are trying to change someone. Write about the costs and benefits of creating this dynamic in a relationship. Who would you be if you let your partners be themselves? Give them the space to be who they are, and refocus on you.

THE ROMANTIC:
I am in love with love, not you.

Annie was a total romantic. On the first date she would imagine having her date's children in Paris. These fantasies took her way into the future so she could not be present to experience the truth of that relationship and her partner's true self.

It is great to love romance, but it is also important to know someone over time. When you put aside the grand gestures and really listen to and observe your partner, you'll find that real, grounded love can be even more personal, profound, and real.

Possible Cause:
Perhaps your family loved passion and drama. You may be someone who is more concerned with ideas of love and beauty than bills and practicality. There are probably many benefits to this idealist approach in your dating life, but the cost is high when they overshadow the reality of your date and situation.

Action:

Make your gestures about your partner, not about love in general. Love your mate as a whole person, not the fantasy that you've made up. Allowing yourself to love fully and realistically will ultimately lead to better choices and experiences.

THE SCROOGE:
This'll never work, so why try?

Irene had given up on men long ago. She characterized them as pigs, cheaters, and sex-crazed maniacs. Anytime she went on a date, she waited to be disappointed. She felt that it was just a matter of time until her date hurt her.

We have all been burned yet most of us continue to hope. Why have you decided that no relationship will work for you? You need to reclaim the positive aspects of relationships that you are not currently seeing. If you expect them to fail, they will fail.

Possible Cause:

Perhaps your parents tended to see the worst in most situations. Ironically, you learned that assuming the worst was the best way of protecting yourself from disappointment. I call this "the other shoe is going to drop" philosophy. You are so worried about potential rejections that it robs you from experiencing any joy in the present.

Action:

Look at the costs and benefits of assuming the worst about things right from the start. Let yourself be happy and hopeful. Look for what is good in all your dates. Keep a list of three daily successes, and catch yourself when you resort to negative thinking. Assume the best for a change.

THE SERIAL MONOGAMIST:
I must always have a partner.

Tonia had always had a boyfriend—she hadn't been single since she was twelve years old. People often wondered if she even knew herself well enough to know what she wanted in a relationship. It seemed like she was lost without a special man in her life because her partner defined her.

We learn from being in long-term relationships, but we also learn from dating and being alone. If your pattern is to go from one long-term relationship to another, ask yourself what it would be like to live an unpartnered life. What might you learn about who you are and what you want?

Possible Cause:

Perhaps you had a close relationship with a parent and learned to share all aspects of your life with another person. Though it is great that you love close relationships, you feel something is wrong when you are alone. This creates uncertainty about whether you can live a satisfying, worthwhile life by yourself.

Action:

Consider whether you want a relationship more than you actually want your particular partner. Then take some time to rediscover your relationship to yourself by participating in activities alone—take a class or go on a private retreat. Learn to trust and like yourself more so you can enter a love-based relationship rather than settling for someone due to feelings of unease or desperation.

THE PLAYER:
I can't commit to just one.
Christine liked the excitement of having a variety of men give her attention; she thrived on being pursued. What really frightened her was the idea that she would let herself get attached to a particular man and then he would hurt her when she was not looking. Her Defensive Dating Style seemed fun (on the surface), but it prevented her from obtaining true intimacy in a committed, long-term relationship.

If you sampled the whole world, you still would not commit to one person. Ask yourself what your fear of having a real relationship is about. Why do you need reinforcement to feel wanted?

Possible Cause:
Maybe your parents had outside relationships or had a hard time committing to things in general. This unstable environment made you emotionally vulnerable growing up, but it was all you knew. Now the idea of a committed relationship scares you.

Action:
Look at the benefits and costs of going from person to person with no constancy. Does this dating style really

work for you? Think about the lack of intimacy in your relationships, and try dating one person for six months. Notice what fears arise; don't run from them. See what it is possible to learn about yourself and the other person from this intimate experience.

Once you have discovered your dating style and how to work on it, begin to approach dating in new ways. If your style is The Control Freak, take a back seat and let your date take the lead for a change. If your style is The Scrooge, practice finding two great things about every date.

You have two choices: Live in fear and remain stuck in your Defensive Dating Style, or practice loving yourself and grow in your ability to love.

Your dating journal is a useful tool in this process. Use it to reflect on how you're moving beyond your Defensive Dating Style and the difference this is making for you.

You can also use this information to recognize your date's defensive style. If he is scared, he may have a style of protecting himself too. Once you understand his style, you will not take his behavior personally. Remember that it is up to him to work through his own fears, but your insight will lead to understanding as you both move toward healthier dating and intimacy. In the next chapter, we'll take a close look at rejection, both receiving it and giving it.

5

YOUR RELATIONSHIP TO "NO": DEALING WITH REJECTION

Trusting someone new can be scary. We are all afraid of rejection, and all of us want to be liked and accepted. Having said this, hearing no is inevitable, in life and in dating. So, the meaning you give to hearing the word will have a dramatic impact on your dating success. As we continue in this section, we will examine what happens to you on a date when you are rejected.

Shelly's story is a perfect example of how to deal with rejection. Shelly went on a date with a man she really liked, and he did not call her again. She then made up a story that no men would like her and that she was a horrible date. Upon further exploration, she realized that after one hour this man could not really know her and that most likely he had decided not to pursue the relationship based on reasons having more to do with him than with her. She accepted this notion and returned to her intention to be herself on her dates until she met the right man who would accept her and stay with her for a lifetime.

In life there is a lot of rejection. Someone will say no to our invitation, to our request for a raise, or to our fundraiser. This does not mean that they do not like us. There are numerous reasons why people say no and most of the reasons are about *them* not you. If you can embrace this new context for rejection, it will free you to go into dating without taking *no* personally. You can be disappointed that you will not be able to continue to get to know a person, but you will not make it define something about you.

Exercise:
Exploring Your Relationship to "No"

Believe it or not, you can make an experience with rejection a productive one. Begin by recalling your last bad date. Remember how it felt when he did not call to ask you out again? How did you interpret this? Did you complain to your friends that nothing works out and that no men like you?

You are not alone. This is the protocol for what happens when a date does not lead to a second one. Rarely do you hear a woman say, "Oh, he did not call again. It's his loss. Next!" and really mean it. We tend to turn the word no into an indictment of ourselves. If you are not sure if you do this, ask your girlfriends. They'll tell you.

If you want to change this and save yourself much dating pain, you need to be honest about your usual reaction to no. What is your first *no* trigger? What do you make it mean? Fill out the following sentences in your dating journal:

- My first reaction to hearing no is:
- When I hear no in dating, I think: (Examples might be "No men like me," "I'll be alone forever," or "It wasn't a good date.")
- The truth could be: (Examples might be "He is afraid of intimacy," "We aren't a good match," or "He met someone else who is a better match.")
- If I could let go of my fear of the word no, it would free me to:

Now that you've been honest about your usual response to being rejected on a date, you can choose to react differently from now on. What will you say about it instead? Here are a few choices:

"The right guy will never leave, so obviously it's not him."

"His loss. I am great."

"It sometimes takes a lot of no to get to the yes in life."

Take a moment to come up with a new reaction to rejection that is healthy and rings true to you. Record it in your dating journal, and commit to saying this to yourself from now on, whenever a date does not work out. It will allow you to move on without making up stories and sabotaging yourself.

WHY YOU SAY "NO" ON DATES

It is also important to look at why you say no on dates. Many daters find something they do not like on the first date and then refuse to go out again. They go through many dates in this way, never taking the time to get to know anybody. In addition, they never let their date know about their concerns, so there is no hope of communication around that issue. For example, Cheryl felt her date talked about himself too much, so she wrote him off. If she had told him about her observation, perhaps he would have been willing to work on it. Sometimes on a first date people talk a lot because they are nervous or afraid of silence. Cheryl's first instinct was to say no to a second date rather than give her date one more chance to explain or to work it out.

Another client of mine went on a date with a man she knew was wonderful as a friend but whom she did not find too attractive. We discussed it, and she decided to continue to get to know him for a few dates. After all, she was free to keep dating other people and so was he. After the first date she said, "He's so great. I wish he were cuter." After the second date she said, "He's a great kisser, but I still can't get past his face." By the fourth date she said, "I find him so sexy. I don't know why I ever thought he was unattractive." Today they are engaged to be married.

Not everyone's story plays out like this, of course. Some people find that physical attraction does not build, but isn't it worth it to find out? I've seen this happen a few times, so I usually recommend giving someone at least three dates if you think they are a nice person. Note that I am not asking you to "settle," but I am suggesting that when you say no, you may be prematurely cutting off a possible mate. Look at when and why you reject your dates so that you can do it consciously—when it truly serves you to do so. If you discover that you tend to say no too quickly, try giving your dates time before you decide if they are right for you.

Hela had strict standards for the man of her dreams. She was tall and wanted her date to be more than an inch taller. I asked her what would happen if she met a fantastic guy who had all her relationship requirements but was an inch shorter. Would she reject that opportunity? Her initial response was "yes." She had been made to feel ugly for being tall in elementary school, and that little girl in her had made a decision to "fit in" by only dating taller men. A twelve-year-old girl was now running the show, and Hela had been missing out on a number of wonderful partners because of an old humiliation. Once she realized this, the mature woman could review her options and create a vision based on her present needs.

The following exercise will help you look at whether you sabotage yourself by saying no too soon or for superficial reasons. It is appropriate and healthy to reject a relationship when it is clear that it will not be a match for you. However, based on what I've observed as a dating counselor, 80 percent of the time when people say no on a first date, it does not fall into that healthy category.

 Exercise:
The Hyper-Rejecter Quiz
To find out if you might be a Hyper-Rejecter, use your dating journal to take the following quiz:

1. Do you decide you are bored on the first date and don't give your date another chance?
2. Do you decide that there is something you do not like on a date and you won't communicate about it?
3. Do you find something wrong with almost every date you meet?
4. Do you decline a second date because you cannot see that you'll ever marry this person?
5. Do you say no to dates much more often than you say yes?

If you have answered yes to any of the above questions, read on.

No one is telling you to marry someone that you are not crazy about, but you should consider why you keep saying no to life and all its possibilities. Sometimes the word no is our protection from being hurt. It keeps you in a narrow box so you don't have to get out and take a risk. Success in dating—like anything—requires openness, a good attitude, and patience. In saying yes to getting to know someone, you are saying yes to learning about yourself in that new relationship. You are agreeing to have a new experience with unlimited possibilities.

This agreement to give dating a chance doesn't mean you can't ever date other people. And it also doesn't mean you should lead someone on or continue torturous dates. I am speaking about those perfectly pleasant dates that get shafted because fireworks don't explode during your first meeting; sometimes chemistry isn't instantaneous. In many happy couples, there is often one person who wasn't exactly blown away by the other when they first initially met. But given time, affection and love were able to flourish and grows into something sustainable. And you can bet these couples are thankful now that they did not hastily turn their back on the possibility of love.

Dating—like life—is not the movies. If you want someone to give you a chance, you need to set the example. What would your life be like if you ventured to say yes a lot more? What if there were no mistakes and everything you learned led you to expand how you could love? Approach your life that way for one month and see what begins to open up. Imagine what it would be like if everything you thought and did supported your intention of meeting your life mate. Do you imagine that you would be sitting home, or would you be out trying to actively meet people?

You probably answered the latter without realizing that your beliefs about love don't support taking necessary action. It has been my experience that many people have beliefs that tell them they can sit around and wait to meet The One. The next section will help you look at whether your past beliefs about dating are sabotaging your success. Be honest about what you usually tell yourself about love, and take a good look at whether it is productive. If you have not been getting the results that you want, it might be time to change your thinking.

FATALIST DATING MYTHS

Many times I hear women complaining that they are thirty-something and don't have a husband. When I ask what they have done about that goal, they usually give me a blank stare. Once in a while they reply, "Shouldn't it just happen? Why do I have to do anything? My friend just met her husband on the subway." My answer is that while it sometimes happens this way, most often it does not. Fairy tales and movies tell us that this is how we'll find love, but these myths do not serve us. The reality is that we need to work at creating what we want in our lives, no matter what it is.

Take Hanna's story, for example. Hanna decided a long time ago that the man of her dreams would ring the doorbell when she least expected it. The trouble was that she had been waiting a long time. Her friends were all getting married and nothing was happening for her! She insisted that online dating was for losers and that it was pathetic to look for love. She desperately wanted to meet someone, but she had taken no action.

Hanna's vision had corresponding actions for her other goals; she just needed to apply this proactive approach to her love life. She reluctantly agreed to try some singles resources, including online dating sites and speed dating services, to increase her chances of finding a mate. Soon she was actively dating and enjoying the process. She cleared her old myth about finding love and was able to create a new possibility by taking action to stand for and create what she most wanted. She became the powerful creator of her own love life rather than a passive bystander.

Take the following quiz to find out if you allow fatalistic dating beliefs to stop you from pursuing your goal of finding a mate.

Exercise:
The Fatalist Dater Quiz: Are You a Fatalist Dater?

Read the following statements and answer "true" or "false" in your dating journal:

1. Finding love should not require effort.
2. It is ridiculous to pay to find love.
3. Love is "meant to be," so you should not have to work on yourself or the relationship.
4. You cannot create opportunities to meet The One.
5. Finding love should not involve rejection. It should be natural and easy.

If you answered that any of the above statements are true, it's time for a reality check.

THE TRUTH ABOUT DATING

1. Love requires effort. Finding a mate may take work—let's face it, even finding yourself does! Telling yourself otherwise makes you passive and puts you at the mercy of your circumstances. Love means getting to know someone and showing you care through your actions; love is a verb. Why shouldn't dating be the same?

2. Payment is a sign of value. You pay to take care of yourself with clothes, makeup, entertainment, relaxation, good food, and so on. Are these things of more value to you than finding a mate? Modern dating services, dating events, and dating coaches are effective and at your fingertips. This belief about not paying to meet someone stops daters from taking advantage of available resources. What is more important than finding a great life mate? Put your money where your mouth is and brainstorm about the resources you can bring to bear. From dating classes and season theater tickets to singles vacations, the possibilities are endless!

3. Love is more than destiny. People who think that love is predestined won't leave their house or lift a finger to meet anyone. It could be that love is predestined, but it could be a long, lonely wait until you meet that person. What are you willing to create in your life in the meantime? Dating gives you experience to learn from. And if love is fate it will happen regardless . . . but what if it's not? Are you willing to put in some effort and take responsibility for the love life you are creating?

4. Life opportunities are created. Based on what you are open to, you create opportunities in life. You create job opportunities by going to school, networking, sending out resumes, interviewing, and getting a career coach. Dating should be no different. If you want a relationship, you need to put yourself in situations where you may meet someone. Take a chance with singles events at church, ask family and friends to fix you up, talk to people at parties and in the grocery store. Think of your daily life as a series of opportunities to meet new people.

5. Many things worth having involve some rejection. Be willing to take risks, learn from the process, and stay committed to your goal. Someone can only reject you if you take it that way. Everyone has the right to say no; the story that you then make up about yourself is your responsibility. In relationships, as well as in everything else in life, we need to be willing to go through the *no* to get to the *yes*.

Given the dating myths that we've just explored, think about how much time and effort you have put into finding your soul mate. Have you tried the classifieds, online dating, dating events, dating coaching and classes, and blind dates? How often? If you told people that you wanted the perfect job but were hoping it would just come to you, you would get some strange looks! We mistakenly think that doing nothing is the best approach when it comes to finding love.

It's true that sometimes people meet out of the blue. Sometimes they are in school, a class, or a job together and they never even formally date. It is fabulous when this happens. But everyone has at least one area in life where things come easily and at least one where they need to work and grow. Consider this an opportunity to learn through your dating experiences, while expanding your own growth.

Exercise:
Rethink Your Dating Beliefs

If you have been taking a fatalist approach to dating, now is the time to take action. Your beliefs about love directly affect your love life because your thoughts determine what you bring into your life. Take a moment now to make a choice: Will you work to find love, pay money to find love, create time to date, and create opportunities to grow in this area of your life? If your past beliefs about dating do not support your best future progress, change them now with an affirmation. Here are a few examples:

- "I will only think, do, and feel things that support me in finding the partner of my dreams."
- "I am willing to work to find a terrific partner."
- "I will make sure that my actions match my words in my love life."

In your dating journal, write a new dating belief that works for you. Remind yourself of it often. It may also be helpful for you to list all of your old fatalist beliefs and set that list on fire. Don't let your old beliefs stop you from creating what you really want in the present and future. Only you get to decide what makes sense and what will be most helpful in your love life. Your thoughts are key.

Congratulations on completing part 1! This is probably the most challenging section for most people. Most of us like to avoid our past, not confront it. At this point you should understand why it is so important to feel complete with your old relationships, models, and fears, so that you can create the relationship of your dreams from a space of lightness, openness, and freedom.

We are now going to close the door on your past and move into the present for part 2. But before we do, I want you to recall the poem "There's a Hole in My Sidewalk" from chapter 1. Remember that change is a gradual process. If at any point you find yourself falling into your old patterns while dating, you can always flip back to this portion of the book for a refresher, and to remind yourself of your present commitment.

In part 2 you will walk into the present with insight and without baggage to create who you want to be in your love life, and in your life at large! From this point on you will view yourself as a powerful creator who takes responsibility for everything exactly as it shows up in your life.

PART 2

BE THE PARTNER YOU WISH TO ATTRACT

6

You Are Who You Date: Attracting Who and What You Create

Often we put a lot of pressure on our dates to be The One. When dates don't live up to our expectations, we degrade the other person to our friends and are left feeling miserable. This is way too much pressure on potential dates! The Law of Attraction states that "like attracts like," so the best strategy is to become the partner you want to meet. Instead of judging yourself and others or waiting for someone to complete you, take responsibility for who *you* are. Then you can consciously choose a partner who is a great match for you. By creating the life that you want, it is in your power to attract the partner of your dreams.

How can you do this? Look at who you are as a date, what you are creating in your life, and what you want to create in your relationships. By taking the focus off of criticizing your dates and putting it on developing your confidence and your self-esteem, you will feel more attractive and powerful in the dating game and everywhere in your life.

This chapter will focus on getting to know yourself better and on becoming more accepting of yourself and others. You may resist this concept because it is much easier to say, "men suck" or to bemoan the fact that "all the good ones are taken." Again I say, if that is your context, that is what will show up for you. It all begins with you and whether you are willing to embrace yourself and do the work to create what you want in your life.

Have fun with these exercises and allow yourself to dream big. This is your life—why not make it everything you have ever wanted? Savor this time as a single person and use it to know yourself and the partner that you want to attract.

SELF-CONFIDENCE

Who you feel you are is projected from the first phone or Internet communication. It gets communicated to your partner in a million ways and has a profound effect on your dating experience—even before you go out! The ability to be clear about who you are and what you want will directly affect the partner you choose. And if you love yourself, you will attract a mate who values you just as much.

Shift your focus from how you would like to be different to cherishing who you are today. Discover how amazing you are and offer your presence fully on every date. The next few exercises will help you own your strengths and accomplishments so you can share them in your relationships.

Exercise:
What Makes You a Great Catch?

Think about why you are a good partner. If you feel negatively about yourself, this will be communicated to your date. Recognizing your own worth will make you aware of how much you have to give.

In your dating journal, make a list of twenty-five things that make you a great date. For example, you could say, "I'm a great listener," "I cook gourmet dinners," "I have a great laugh," or "I'm fluent in three languages." Review your list of fabulous attributes before every date, and you will begin to vibrate confidence and radiance on all your dates.

YOUR ACCOMPLISHMENTS: WHAT MAKES YOU A STAR?

Think about a time when you were on stage and all eyes were on you. Picture your mom, sitting in the third row, with tears in her eyes because she was so proud of you. Everyone was clapping. You knew that you made an impact and people appreciated you.

This is so often opposite to the feelings that come up when we are dating. We feel judged, useless, uninteresting, and worse—when it is not at all the reality. We all have gifts and triumphs, and it is important to recognize your achievements and feel the sense of pride that you deserve. Reminding yourself in tangible ways that you are a winner will reaffirm that you can also create a successful relationship because you have a lot to offer. This will also help when dating seems tough and you need something positive to share about yourself. I am not talking about bragging. It is simply recognizing your strengths and accomplishments so you can draw upon that feeling of appreciation for yourself. It will also give you practice in looking for those types of things in your dates.

There is nothing to be gained by not accepting yourself. Where there is judgment there cannot be love. You cannot expect someone to love you until you love yourself. You will always have things that you wish to change about yourself and so will your dates. Does that mean you are not loveable now? Many of my clients feel they are not "dateable" until they lose weight, get rid of their panic attacks, or fix other things that they consider flaws, but this self-rejection is bound to become a self-fulfilling prophecy.

One of my clients decided that she could never date, get married, or be a mother because of her psychiatric disorder, even though she managed her condition well. With some coaching, she learned to accept that this was one part of her. Once she changed her opinion of herself, she began dating a man whom she married within a year. She now sees no problem in becoming a mother. What changed was her acceptance of herself.

Self-love is a process that starts by becoming aware of how you disown yourself. The next exercises will guide you through this.

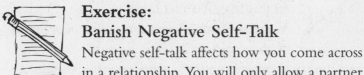

Exercise:
Banish Negative Self-Talk

Negative self-talk affects how you come across in a relationship. You will only allow a partner to love you as much as you love yourself. Remember, neither you nor your partner will ever be perfect. The best relationships are between two people who accept themselves and each other.

To do this exercise, first ask yourself what you don't like about yourself and why and then record your answers in your dating journal. For example:

- I'm overweight—makes me feel unattractive
- I'm shy—makes me more self-conscious
- I don't know about politics—makes me feel stupid
- I can't cook—makes me feel that a man would be disappointed

Now ask yourself what makes you feel that you are not a good date and record those answers.

Look at both of your lists and determine what you are willing to change or accept. For each item on your lists, write next to it how you will either work to change it or come to accept it. For example:

- I am controlling—
  makes me feel mean → Allow myself to be open
  Have compassion
  for myself

Commit to accepting yourself today because it will affect all that you do in your life.

Exercise:
Accepting Your Dates

As I've mentioned, you can only accept others to the extent that you accept yourself. You have probably already gotten a sense of whether you are a Hyper-Rejecter from the previous chapter. If you are a Hyper-Rejecter, this exercise will be especially useful to you. Even if you are not a Hyper-Rejecter, the practice will remind you to be accepting and positive on every date.

After each date, fill out answers to the following questions in your dating journal. Notice if this activity changes your attitude and the success of your dating life.

1. What are your date's strengths?
2. What was good about the experience?
3. What did you learn about your date?
4. What did you learn about yourself?
5. What positive feedback/appreciation did you give?
6. How were you generous? How was your date generous?
7. Did you find anything in common? If so, what?

SELF-ESTEEM

I see it all the time in my practice: women believing that finding a partner will make them feel good about themselves and validate them. While it is satisfying to have a special person who loves you, that never fixes what you really feel about yourself, deep down; only you can address that.

It all begins with the degree to which you like yourself, and having self-esteem involves making yourself a priority and treating yourself with love. When this comes naturally to you, you can't help but attract a mate who will treat you with the same love, kindness, and respect that you give yourself.

Lara was beautiful, smart, and kind. She came across as shy and described herself as boring. As we worked on this, she realized that she was not being fair to herself. She had always wanted to take a cooking class and a voice class. She decided to do these things for herself, not for a man. By pursuing her goals, she began to enjoy her life more, which was contagious to her dates. Soon she had three men who wanted her to become exclusive with them, but she took her time and got to know each of them before closing off her dating options. Externally, there was no major change in Lara; what changed was the way she saw herself and valued her life.

It is important to take risks and let your true self shine through. This creates intimacy, authenticity, and learning. Identifying where you are holding back in your life will allow you to address the problem area and embrace risk-taking. As you become more comfortable revealing who you are, people who are aligned with you will be attracted. This is a great way to ensure that you attract someone who is a true match for you.

In the upcoming exercises we are going to look at your relationship to yourself—how you treat yourself, trust yourself, reveal yourself, and enjoy your own company. You will experience what you love about who you are, and you will notice the thoughts and feelings you try to escape. Through this process of identifying how you love and reject yourself, you will learn to further know and accept yourself.

Exercise:
Assess Your Self-Esteem
In your dating journal, record your answers to the following questions:

1. Do you take time for yourself on a regular basis?
2. Do you focus on the good in life more than the bad?
3. Do you focus on the good *in you* more than the bad?
4. Do you take time for self-care?
5. Do you spend at least 75 percent of your energy on things you want to do (rather than things you "should" do)?
6. Are you motivated to please yourself more than pleasing others?
7. Do you love yourself despite outside circumstances?
8. Do you make sure that you eat, sleep, rest, have fun, and meet your needs?
9. Do you feel responsible for all that you create in your life?
10. Do you make time to do what you love and to express your gifts?

If you answered no to any of the questions, spend some time reflecting on that issue. What keeps you from doing this? Read on for some ideas about taking regular time to love yourself.

WAYS TO ADDRESS YOUR SELF-ESTEEM

How much you love yourself begins with your thoughts and how you treat yourself. We have already begun to help you see yourself through the eyes of love. Now let's address specific action steps that you can take to treat yourself really well.

Care for Yourself:
Begin to practice self-care on a regular basis. Take walks in the park, get a manicure/pedicure, take yourself to the movies, buy yourself some beautiful flowers. Do things that make you feel great and know you deserve it!

Please Yourself:
Think about how often your motivation is to please others instead of yourself. If pleasing others is your priority, begin to choose differently. Putting yourself first once in a while is necessary for your emotional well-being. You need to refuel before you can give.

Weigh the "Want" Against the "Should":
Consider how often you do activities because you should or because it looks good. Start to think about what you really *want to do* and try that instead. Let go of any guilt you associate with not accomplishing what you "should," and allow yourself to enjoy your true desires.

Practice Appreciation and Gratitude:
Look at what's positive in your life, and journal about it. Remember that what you focus on expands. Find at least

three things you appreciate daily. If they are about you (instead of outside of you) you get extra points!

Challenge Your Inner Gremlin:

Talk back to the critic in your head. Don't let it wreak havoc on your self-confidence and self-esteem. Challenge that negative voice with affirmations about what is good in you and that situation.

Take Responsibility:

You are the creator of your life, not the victim. Take responsibility for what you attract, and you will feel empowered to direct your life's trajectory.

Accept Yourself:

Work on accepting all parts of you without judgment. Love yourself completely.

Recognize Your Strengths:

Affirm your strengths and develop them. If you love guitar, go to a park and play for some friends. Find something you love and share it. Websites like meetup.com and craigslist.org are great resources for meeting other people in your area who share your interests. Explore different ways to pursue your passions while meeting new faces.

Share Your Gifts:

Use your talents in the world, and step out of your comfort zone to reveal your true self. You never know who might be watching and falling in love with the real you.

Volunteer:

Let who you are make a difference to someone else. This will remind you of how valuable you are in relationships.

Develop Yourself:

Going to therapy or coaching is a great way to begin to love and accept yourself within the context of a relationship. You do not have to be depressed, mentally ill, or in crisis to benefit from this opportunity.

Practice Commitment:

When you are consistently good to yourself and your actions match your words, you begin to trust yourself. This kind of follow-through is excellent for your self-esteem.

Become Your Own Best Friend:

Tend to your needs, whether you are sick, sad, or in the mood to celebrate. Make time for things that are important to you and honor them no matter what.

How you feel about yourself is communicated immediately. So before you form a great relationship with someone else, work on having a wonderful lifelong relationship with yourself. When you feel happy, healthy, peaceful, fulfilled, and centered things tend to come to you more easily. They become an added pleasure—not a necessity—and you become even more attractive.

7

FALL IN LOVE WITH YOU: LOVE YOURSELF AND ATTRACT EVEN MORE LOVE

If you had ten minutes to tell someone all the positive things about you, could you and would you? My experience with clients is that most of them have all their faults right at the tip of their tongue, but only a lot of "Ummms..." when I ask for a list of their strengths. They often feel humble and embarrassed about singing their own praises and often have to ask coworkers, friends, and family for help in making a list. You can learn to be proud of who you are and have a sense of humor about sharing it. We will practice that in this chapter.

Own Up to Your Strengths

It would be outrageously refreshing if everyone listed his or her gifts on a business card and handed them out at singles events. I developed this strategy and suggest it to my clients as a fun way for them to get attention and start conversations. The reaction I usually get from this idea is fear and hesitation: daters fear that people will think that they are full of themselves if they hand out a card that says how they are great. Just because you know your own worth, doesn't mean you are stuck-up or unbalanced.

Can you imagine a guy sorting through a fistful of cards from a speed dating event and coming across yours? It's bound to make him smile. "What a nice change to meet a woman who knows she is a catch and has a terrific sense of humor and playfulness!" he'll think. "Why not call her and see?" There are major payoffs when you learn to exploit your strengths.

 Exercise:
Create Your Dating Calling Card
On a card the size of a business card, write down all the reasons why someone would be lucky to date you, and don't be shy!

Remember to add your name and phone number because a card like this is likely to pique the interest of quite a few potential dates. See the example on the next page.

Even if you think you're too shy to give out a card that sings your praises, go ahead and make it anyway. You can always keep the card secretly in your wallet, so you will smile and feel more confident knowing it is there. And

Courageous, beautiful, funny, smart, kind, interesting, a student, teacher, coach, friend, family-oriented, romantic, visionary, writer, speaker, generous, creative, unique, surprising, nature lover, loves kids, traveler, spiritual, analytical, curious, open, insightful, goal-oriented, responsible, hard-working, confident, honest, direct, compassionate, inspiring, fun, charismatic, powerful, successful, artistic, whimsical, loyal, a person of integrity, sexy, authentic . . . **AND SINGLE!**

☎ *(123) 456-7890*

FIGURE 3: Personal Calling Card

this is not about gimmicks or "appearing" a certain way. It's all about really owning who you are, being proud, and connecting with your own power. Remember that any guy would be lucky to have the chance to get to know you.

LIKING YOUR OWN COMPANY

Another way to improve your relationship with yourself is to spend some quality time with you! So many of my clients constantly keep busy "doing" or surrounding themselves with parties or friends. When they sit alone to watch a movie they feel like a loser, or buried negative feelings surface. These feelings are not something to run from. Look deeper into them, so they can be understood and released. If you are sad, allow yourself to cry and later journal about it. See if you can accept whatever is going on with you, with love and compassion. Then you will be able to love and be with yourself no matter where you are or who you are with.

It is great to be social and active, but when you are also able to sit still and be loving with yourself, you can be happy without needing anything more. Another person can join you in this authentic, peaceful space, and neither of you have to be busy, impressive, or fake. When you really like your own company, your need for outside approval decreases.

Ask yourself this: Do you like your own company? Can you regularly spend an evening by yourself just doing the things that give you pleasure? Many of my clients run from one bad relationship to the next because they cannot be alone. Being with someone who treats them badly feels better then being with themselves.

When you can be with yourself without feeling anxious or bored, it is easier to be authentic and present with another person. Time alone—with stillness instead of distractions—allows you to connect with your feelings and confront them. By looking within, you can know what is there and deal with it. That frees you up to give another person your attention and be totally present in the situation. It also allows you to continue loving yourself no matter what the other person does.

It is also important to discover your interests and passions, because having your own life gives you something to share in a relationship and makes you less likely to depend on your partner to fulfill all your needs. This takes pressure off the relationship.

Many women move in packs. When they don't have a boyfriend, they are surrounded by girlfriends. Most can't tell you the last date they had with themselves! Other than getting a manicure/pedicure. They don't look forward to walking in the park, going to a museum, or seeing a movie alone. Being by themselves seems like the worst possible fate. If this is the case, why should a great guy want to spend time with you?

In order to master being a good date—to know yourself, like yourself, and enjoy your company—you need to regularly date yourself! It may take some discipline and commitment at first, but many of my clients find that after it becomes a habit, they wouldn't give it up for anything. This is what we are going to work on in the next exercise.

A word of warning: Don't go into this exercise with a lot of expectations. Just pick something that you love to do (at least) every two weeks, mark a day on your calendar with a heart, and make it your day. The trick is to keep it sacred and not to cancel on yourself when "something better" comes along!

Instead of focusing on your partner, you need to experience yourself as a date. What feelings come up when you're alone? Are you bored? Sad? Do you like your own company? After each date, fill out a "Date Yourself Record Form" in your journal and see what you learn from the experience. For example:

Date: *March 17*
Activity: *Went to Long Wood Garden*
Feelings: *Felt sad and self-critical*
Thoughts: *I am not good enough.*
What I learned: *I am too hard on myself.*

Root cause: *My mom was critical.*
Action taken: *Look at the positives more*
What I accomplished: *Self-reflection and understanding*
How this will affect my relationships: *I will like myself more and will be more positive with others.*

Exercise:
Rate Your Self-Acceptance Level

In the process of dating, you will experience rejection. Remember that the trick is to avoid rejecting yourself in the process. Read the following statements. For each one, see if you agree or disagree and write your answers in your dating journal.

1. When a date doesn't like me, I do not blame myself.
2. I accept myself as I am.
3. Any man would be lucky to have me.
4. I spend more time complimenting rather than criticizing myself.
5. I have created a life I love.
6. I feel comfortable being alone.
7. I don't wait for a partner to come before I experience the things I want.
8. I have a support network of people who treat me well.
9. If nothing in my life changed, I would still be happy.
10. I could easily compose a list of my twenty-five personal strengths.

If you disagree with more than two statements in the above exercise, you need to boost your self-acceptance. You may decide to try therapy to work on this issue. Read on for some more ideas.

Reveal Yourself

One way to increase your self-acceptance is to reveal yourself in your life. Start embracing all of who you are now and share it.

Carol was private and self-conscious. She came across on her dates as very guarded, and she often worried that people would judge her. In order to change this, she took some baby steps. She joined a book group and shared her ideas. She began to make herself speak up more at work meetings and took opportunities to share deeper parts of herself with friends and family. This process of opening up was scary at first, but she saw that nothing bad happened to her. In fact, she felt more confident, relaxed, and comfortable in her own skin. Over time, she was more present and open on her dates. She met men who liked her for who she was, and they found her to be interesting, open, and fun.

To attract the right person for you, you have to come out of your shell. Start doing things you always wanted to do but were too afraid to try. And take opportunities to become the person you always wanted to be. Don't worry if you make mistakes along the way.

Exercise:
Seizing Moments to Reveal Yourself
It's time to accomplish what you want in life, but you need to face your fears. In your dating journal, write down the risks you've always wanted to take (writing a book, pursuing acting, traveling to a foreign country, etc.), what has kept you from taking them, what

you will change, and the lesson you expect to learn from taking that leap.

Build self-confidence by defining your fears and taking a chance. This always has a domino effect in the other areas of your life. When you reveal your true self, you inspire others to do the same. This is true of potential dates and even existing relationships with friends and family. And dating requires that you open up to new people and be yourself.

When you love yourself for who you really are and have others who feel that way about you too, it becomes easier not to take rejection personally. In any aspect of life, all you can do is your part. You can't control other people, the weather, the circumstances, the competition, the judges, or the outcome. All you can do is take a flying leap and learn from the experience. So really take some time to look at what has stopped you. Then take a leap of faith, and live the life of your dreams, now.

8

COMMIT TO YOUR LIFE VISION: BUILDING THE IDEAL LIFE SO THE IDEAL MATE WILL FOLLOW

YOUR LIFE VISION

Now that we have looked at who you are in your life, let's turn our attention to the life you are currently living. Your life is a reflection of what you are committed to. Many women feel that their life will start when The One shows up. Only then will they go on vacation, buy a house, or take ballroom dancing lessons. Meanwhile, they feel unhappy and incomplete, or at the very least stalled. These women hope to attract a relationship from this place of scarcity and need. Think of

the relationship they could create from a space of abundance, satisfaction, responsibility, self-love, and fulfillment!

One way to radiate these qualities is to seize your dreams and create everything you want NOW! Begin to live every moment to the fullest and you will attract your match. In my practice, a potential partner often enters when my clients are actively engaged in something they are passionate about and are having lots of fun in their lives. When I was dating, I taught an adjunct graduate class that I loved teaching. My class really participated, and we had a great time. The director came in a few times to watch and told me how much the students loved me. Eventually, he asked me out; we had teaching in common. Similarly, I met my husband at a clinic where we shared a family therapy case. I had the brother in individual treatment and he had the sister in therapy. We both worked with their mother and really cared about the family, and this mutual concern brought us an awareness of each other. Partners often share a similar core energy, so doing the things that you love can be one great way to attract a like-minded person.

In the following exercises, you will examine your Life Vision, Life Satisfaction, and Action Plan. This will allow you to take responsibility for everything that shows up in your life and remind you that you can create your dreams through vision and action. This includes your dream of creating an ideal relationship.

Exercise:
What Is Your Life Vision?

Why wait until you're part of a couple to pursue your dreams? If you create the life you love, you will be more likely to attract the man who will fit into it. The first step is becoming clear about your life vision by making a collage of it. Some people also call these vision boards or treasure maps. Whatever you call yours, it will be a useful tool as you make your life vision a reality.

Take a stack of magazines while you are watching your favorite show or movie, and cut out any pictures or images that speak to you. Put them in an envelope, and don't over-analyze the process; just allow your heart to choose. Then buy a posterboard from your local drugstore or stationary store, some glue sticks, and markers. Glue your pictures onto your poster board, and add any inspirational words or sym-bols that represent the creative energy you are going to manifest in your life. Your unconscious communicates in images (like your dreams), so creating a visual picture of what you want to manifest is very powerful. Hang it somewhere special in your home where you see it daily to inspire you.

Here are some life categories that you can capture in your collages:

Location   Family   Career   Relationships   Mission

The next step is to journal about your Life Vision and put in to words what you wish to achieve in these different areas of your life. With your vision recorded in both words and images, you are that much closer to manifesting your dreams. You become clear about your desires, and your unconscious obliges by working with you to achieve them.

As you actively set in motion the forces that will bring about your vision, you will see that you don't need a man to come save you and create your life. Instead you can

FIGURE 4: Life Vision Board

choose a man with a phenomenal life to share in yours. Then he will already know who you are by what you have created. Many women try to adjust to the man they are with, giving up what they want and then blaming him for it later. This stance puts too much pressure on the relationship and does not empower you. The responsibility is yours, so get busy making your vision a reality!

Exercise:
Translate Your Vision into Action

This exercise will help you pinpoint how to take steps to create the life of your dreams now. Be patient with yourself. You may need a long-term plan to save for the house of your dreams, but you would be surprised by how good it feels to put away $1 a day and then see how your consistent commitment and action soon creates something tangible. The point is to take steps to manifest your vision starting today.

You need to translate your vision into action by breaking it down into concrete steps that you can tackle. Begin by choosing a dream from one of the life categories in the last exercise. Then write in your dating journal about the obstacles to that dream and the action needed to overcome them. Do this for each dream or goal that makes up your life vision. For example:

WISH: *"I'd love to buy a house, but maybe I should wait till I'm married . . ."*
OBSTACLES: *Fear, lack of real estate know-how, distrust of self, huge responsibility*
ACTION TAKEN: *Consult real estate ads, attend open houses, look for good repair people, ask support network for help, look for a mortgage, get a broker. Gather information and resources and then you will be clear about the excuses you tell yourself and what can be done about it.*

How Satisfied Are You with Your Life?

It is common to wait for a mate to arrive and make us happy. How attractive is that from the other person's perspective? Would you like to marry an unhappy man and then try to improve his life? Or would you rather be inspired by who he is right now and think, "Wow, I'd like to share this! Sign me up"? When you make the most of what you have and who you are, you make room for even more abundance. In this section, I am asking you to really look at and admit how satisfied you are in the different areas of your life so you can begin to take responsibility for improving them.

Measuring Your Happiness

To do this exercise, use your dating journal to rate your satisfaction in the following life areas from 0 to 10, with 0 being not at all satisfied and 10 being completely satisfied. For each answer, explain why.

Fun/Leisure
Family
Social relationships
Intimate relationships
Spirituality
Health
Career
Finances
Self-care
Life action plan

Don't stop with writing in your journal! Take action now to improve any areas that lack complete satisfaction. For example, if your intimate relationships are a 2, how can you move them to a level 3 this week? You can go out to a few singles events and meet new prospects. Create an action plan to improve your satisfaction in each life area, including dates and benchmarks. The more you put your dreams into action, the stronger your self-confidence and life satisfaction will be.

ASSESS YOUR LEVEL OF COMMITMENT

Changing anything involves much commitment and dedication. How is your commitment level? Do you follow through on the things that you say you will do? When you show a strong level of commitment to areas such as work and health, there's a good chance that you will apply that same level of commitment to dating and relationships. You must practice committing to the things you value in order to be a powerful creator.

Take Mandy's story. Mandy came to my office with complaints about her wishy-washy, commitment-phobic boyfriend of two years. I reminded her that we were there to work on her, and she seemed stunned. She thought about my premise that you attract who you are and said, "But I am really responsible. I do what I say I will do." On the surface, her statement seemed true. She was reliable at work and generally showed up for her appointments. However, when it came to anything surrounding the man she was dating, she was not committed to her word. For instance, she would tell him that she would not tolerate him continuing to keep her waiting all night, yet if he stood her up and went to a bar instead, she would go to that bar to be with him. Then she said that she wanted him to respect her.

When Mandy was in this relationship, her word went out the window and her date ran the show. Mandy had been complaining about her date's lack of commitment instead of seeing that she wasn't being true to her word. Once she was able to see this, Mandy's life began to change. She broke up with her boyfriend and started dating two other men who treated her well. Over time, she learned to honor her word and commitments regardless of what her date was doing. As a result, she eventually partnered with a responsible, caring man who treated her as she deserved to be treated, and who mirrored her good treatment of herself.

 Exercise:
How Committed Are You?
In your dating journal, break down each of the important areas of your life into the three categories that follow and note where you lack commitment and what you could do about it. For example:

HEALTH

Committed to: Working out three times a week
Commitment level: Not so good
Corrective action: Will get a trainer twice a week and document my progress

Do this for all the different areas of your life, including work, family, finances, relationships, dating, hobbies, self-development, and spiritual development. See where you lack commitment and begin to address it.

When my client Judy did this exercise, she found that she had high levels of satisfaction in her work and her finances. She had a high-powered job that took up most of her time. She felt dissatisfied in the areas of dating and fun and decided that she needed to make some changes. She hired someone to help with household chores and began to delegate at work. She also left work by 6 PM and kept her weekends free. Then she used her leftover time on nights and weekends to address her fun and dating goals.

Her life became much more balanced as she committed to increasing her dating prospects and participating in things she really enjoyed and that mattered to her.

COMMITMENT TO SELF

Many women want to be married before they have "married" themselves. The basis of marriage is that you commit to be there for someone else no matter what happens. You don't know what the future holds, but you vow to deal with sickness and adversity while honoring and cherishing the other person. Why won't we do this for ourselves?

When things are going great, we like ourselves just fine. But when we gain twenty pounds, lose a job, or have a bad dating spell, we become our own worst enemies. Commitment means that we do not turn our back on ourselves when things get tough. It means that we stick with it for the long haul, despite mistakes.

Now is the time to assess and address your level of commitment to your life. Knowing where you stand will help you to practice the discipline of following through on things when it is uncomfortable, unpleasant, or inconvenient—an important skill for success in any long-term relationship or goal.

Defining your level of commitment to yourself will affect your dating success. For example, if you commit to a life of treating yourself with respect and then you fall in love with an alcoholic who wants you to give up your career, you will need to choose whether you commit to him or yourself. The best relationships are an extension of our commitment to ourselves because they honor who we are and what we stand for. If both people commit to this context, they will truly accept one another and can create a shared vision.

WOULD YOU MARRY YOURSELF?

Assess your level of commitment to yourself by asking this: Would you marry yourself as you are right now? Would you choose your own company and partnership for the rest of your life? Be honest about your answer.

If your answer is no, why did you respond this way? Do you not have your finances under control? Is your temper too fiery? Are you ready to be a mother? Are you able to make the commitments that marriage requires? None of us is perfect. We are all "works in progress" but it's important to identify where you are not marriageable if you wish to manifest marriage. Identify your own apprehension so you can address it. For example, if you need to work on getting ready to be a mother, you could get a dog to learn how to care for someone other than yourself. Use your dating journal to keep track of your apprehensions and your solutions for dealing with them. Once you have addressed them, it's time to consider to what degree you will commit to yourself.

Exercise:
Get Engaged to Yourself

I often see that my dating clients are not ready to get married because they have not yet married themselves. They do not accept themselves and do not know what they most want in life, so they cannot commit to either. When a client does not have clear standards and a vision to which she is committed, she is susceptible to choosing a life partner based on unconscious feelings or attraction. For this reason, I recommend that my clients first clarify what they intend to create in their lives and then find a partner who supports it.

I've developed a ritual of marrying yourself because it is something that we don't celebrate in our society. The happy ending is all about finding the other person, but often the precursor to that is choosing yourself. Once you make a commitment to yourself, you will immediately be less lonely and more focused.

Create your own engagement ritual in your dating journal or refer to my script below, performing either when you feel ready. For the ceremony that follows you will need nine roses of your favorite color and pomegranate seeds. Let the ceremony remind you of your intention to love and accept yourself fully, and vow to commit to what you want to create.

"I am here today with the intention to propose to myself. I will throw roses into the ocean to signify my commitment to this process. I know I won't be perfect, but I will remember this ceremony as a symbol of my vow to develop my lifelong commitment to myself.

*"The first rose symbolizes **Love**, the most important thing I want in the person I marry. I will apply this commitment by really loving myself, no matter what life brings, which means relying on myself, comforting myself, and honoring who I am in my life choices.*

*"The next rose symbolizes **Responsibility**. This means growing into a person who matches words with actions, is*

trustworthy, practices self-awareness, and follows through on commitments.

"The third rose symbolizes **Finances**. I don't need a wealthy partner, but I desire someone who can basically care for himself. He should have a plan for how to stay within the reality of his means so that I feel like he has control over his situation. I will make a budget and a short—and long-term financial plan that will create the kind of practical security required for the life I want.

"The fourth rose symbolizes **Caring for Myself**. In order to take good care of someone else, I need to first take good care of myself. This applies also to eating reasonably, exercising, getting regular check-ups, managing time in a healthy way, and keeping my environment beautiful so that I am energetically at my best.

"The fifth rose symbolizes **Caring for Others**. Before I choose to have a child, I want a pet to practice putting the welfare of another living being first, no matter what happens. In a long-term love relationship there will be good times and challenges, and I need to be prepared for both.

"The sixth rose represents **Accepting and Cherishing**. I want a partner who does not want to change who I am and who can fully embrace me. In order to attract that, I need to do that within myself first. This means addressing things that I don't like about myself and accepting the things that I can't change. It also means realizing that I am loveable just the way I am so that I can approach others with the same kind of acceptance.

"The seventh rose symbolizes **Creating a Life**. I want a partner who already has a life to share, including a job,

*good friends, clear values, and a life vision. In the mean-
time, I will save money and create a plan to reach my goals,
instead of waiting for a future mate to make it happen.*

*"The eighth rose symbolizes **Encouragement**. I want
someone who believes in me, sees my passion, and helps me
to grow. I need to foster my own dreams, whatever they may
be. I cannot put my dreams ahead of my partner's dreams
because I want a relationship with room enough for both of
our dreams.*

*"The last rose symbolizes **Trust**. Being trustworthy to
myself and others requires the ability to keep my own coun-
sel and live with integrity. I want to work on speaking my
truth and trusting my intuition so that I make choices
aligned with my Higher Self.*

*"I will now eat Persephone's pomegranate seeds. By eat-
ing pomegranate seeds, Persephone was bound to returning
to the underworld for a part of every year. This was painful,
but it enabled her journey into her unconscious—into the
parts of herself that she could not see or explore before—in
order to become whole. This was her individuation, her marriage to herself. She then understood hidden parts of herself
and could make conscious choices. In honor of Persephone, I
consume and release this seed, sending my intention out into
the Universe in the belief that it will grow."*

Exercise:
Marry Yourself

Once you get engaged to yourself, take the
next step—have a wedding ceremony! Go to
the beach or some other significant location and declare
that you are ready to marry yourself. List what you want in

your life and how you will support yourself in getting it. Include any vows or props that are important to you. Following is an example of a marriage ceremony script. To do it you will need a bouquet of white roses and a ring to symbolize your commitment to yourself.

"I am here today to marry myself. I will throw roses into the ocean to signify my commitment to myself from this moment on. I accept myself fully and stand for who I am, and make choices in alignment with that. I promise to love, cherish, and accept myself in sickness and in health. I honor my life vision and take responsibility for all that I create and live.

"In my relationship vision I have a partner who is kind, spiritual, fun, romantic, responsible, committed, and wise. I am this kind of partner for him. I will honor my ability to create this type of partnership.

"The values I am committed to embodying in my life include a life full of love, compassion, inspiration, peace, and joy.

"This ring symbolizes my wholeness and commitment now. I am complete and inspired to create a wonderful, loving life from this moment on—a life I will share with everyone I touch."

By now you know that there is no way to choose the proper partner until you choose yourself; only then is it possible to know your match. In this chapter you have embraced yourself, created the life you want, and committed to what is most important to you going forward. This means that you will put these things first in anything that you do. And when you start to actively date (in part 3), you will be willing to walk away from a great, sexy guy if he goes against or disregards what you most want in your life. You are now clear on your core values and vision, so commit to not selling yourself short or lying to yourself out of fear.

Having said this, no partner is perfect, and all have some issues or foibles. Just be honest and compassionate about what you can live with without giving up the most important things that you have just committed to.

PART 3

CONSCIOUS
DATING

9

Date While You Are Awake: Setting Clear Intentions to Create What You Want

Welcome to part 3, where we will focus on creating conscious relationships in the present. You have put your old relationships in their place and have strengthened your relationship to yourself. Now you will practice dating while wide awake so that you are not completely derailed by your unconscious matchmaker, old baggage, your date's charm, or your immediate and powerful feelings. In this section you will assess your priorities, set your intentions, hone your relationship skills, and create your own Dating Action Plan.

This is where your clarity and your commitment to your vision will be put into action. You will date many wonderful people and will have a great time in the process. The key is to know yourself well enough to know who is a match for you!

YOUR DATING KARMA

Remember that you will learn from everyone you meet. Sometimes you will learn something about a new profession or hobby, and other times you will just enjoy meeting a first-rate person. Even if your date is not the best romantic fit, make the most of every experience. Being conscious in dating not only means picking well; it means behaving well. So treat your dates as you would like to be treated. Be courteous and positive and make the other person feel good for having taken their time to meet you. This creates good dating karma, which leaves people better than you found them for knowing you. And not every experience has to end in a romantic relationship or marriage. When I was dating, I developed a few male friends who were not romantic matches, and they are still good friends with my husband and me. Two even attended our wedding.

You will meet people along your dating path who enrich your life in ways that you don't expect. They might invite you to a party, introduce you to a new friend, give you a terrific business idea, or turn you on to a new kind of music. Be open to the possibilities—even if it is just a one-time meeting—and look for something wonderful about the person before you.

Exercise:
Your Conscious Want Ad

In an earlier chapter, you wrote your Unconscious Want Ad based on the pattern of men that you had been attracting. Now that you have made those old patterns conscious, it's time to write your Conscious Want Ad. What do you most want in a partner? How do you want your partner to treat you? What kind of values would you like your partner to have?

Write your Conscious Want Ad in your dating journal, and feel free to be as descriptive as you want. Give it a lot

WANTED.
A man who is committed,
able to express his feelings,
differentiated from his
family of origin, generous,
and responsible.

FIGURE 5: Personal Ad

109

of thought and choose carefully. A friend of mine created a want ad and attracted a man who fit the description to a tee. (Her only regret was that she didn't include "he's unmarried"!)

It helps to consider the opposite of your Unconscious Want Ad for contrast.

Remember to phrase your want ad in positive words instead of "not" something. In the example on the preceeding page (Figure 5), we are asking for a man who is "differentiated from his family of origin" instead of saying "not a mama's boy." Using clear, positive language will bring about the best results.

Exercise:
What's Not Negotiable?

It's fun to ask the Universe for qualities of your ideal mate, such as a love for house chores. But it is important to be clear about which qualities are necessities and which are bonuses. You don't want to disqualify a potential date because he fits everything in your want ad except the "sharp dresser" part. Therefore, take some time to decide which seven qualities you cannot live without in a mate and then write these in your dating journal.

You do not want this list to be too long (or you'll be too picky) or too short (or you will haphazardly get into any relationship). With each quality you choose, be concrete. For example, I wanted kindness in a husband. This quality means different things to different people. How did I know that my husband was kind? Many men act charming in the beginning of courtship. We worked at the same clinic and were out on a lunch break. My now husband asked me for a quarter, pointing out that the meter in front of us was about to expire. I said, "I thought your car was over there by the clinic." He said, "It is but that person is about to get a ticket." It stunned me that he was so caring about a stranger. There were other things like him pressing "lobby" in the elevator when we were going to the seventeenth floor, so that someone entering the building had an elevator waiting; and the way he was with his family and friends. Get the idea?

I want you to be concrete about what you most want in a person, why, and how you will recognize it. This will help you to most effectively recognize and choose your partner.

Then ask yourself: How often have your past partners met or not met these criteria? Now that you are clear on the qualities that are most important, you will more easily recognize these important qualities in your potential partners and know sooner if they are the right match for you.

Knowing what you want in a relationship isn't the only thing you need to be clear about as you move forward. Be mindful of where you went astray before and what you won't accept in a relationship now. You also have to consider your needs and the sacrifices that might be required of you. Dating and exploring is fun but so is your free time. Having a relationship requires time, money, energy, and compromise. What are you willing to give up in order to have what you want? Now is the time to get straight if you truly desire to have the relationship of your dreams and what you are willing to do about it.

WHAT WON'T YOU ACCEPT?

We all need to know our standards. Think about what is unacceptable to you in a relationship so that you do not spend too much time on the wrong one. Some examples might involve dating someone lazy, someone who won't let you work, someone who is physically or emotionally abusive, someone who doesn't want kids, someone who can't commit, or someone who is a drug addict, a liar, or a cheater. Take some time to ponder these and write them in your dating journal. If you're clear about what you won't accept, you'll have better luck avoiding these pitfalls the next time you encounter them.

Sophie was forty years old and really wanted a child. She craved for a man who wanted to move in with her, but he already had kids and did not want any more. As hard as it was, Sophie ended this relationship instead of getting in even deeper and hoping to change his mind. Staying with him would interfere with her goal of having biological kids of her own.

Exercise:
Assessing Your Sacrifices and Gains

As wonderful as relationships are, there are things that you may have to give up in order to have what you truly want. Tanya had a great life. She was independent and social, and liked to do whatever she wanted whenever she wanted. She liked her space and did not want to be told what to do. At the same time, she wanted marriage and children. She had to examine what she was willing to sacrifice, determine whether she was ready, and calculate the cost required to gain the relationship of her dreams. Otherwise she would sabotage her success and/or resent her partner.

By looking at the risk/benefit ratio of getting your dream relationship, you are making a conscious, responsible decision about whether it is worth the effort to have a lifetime mate. What are you willing to give up for the relationship of your dreams? It can be feelings, beliefs, lifestyle, fears, tangible things, etc. Use your dating journal to make a list similar to the one listed here and elaborate upon each thing and what it means to you:

Judgments
Single life
Cautiousness
Being right
Time alone
Space
Other dating possibilities

For everything you give up, you'll be able to gain something even better when you achieve the relationship you want. Next, write all of the wonderful things you gain and give in a great relationship. Focus on these, and begin to see them as your current reality. The energy created by your thoughts and feelings will attract this reality to you. Make the conscious choice that it is worth it.

RELATIONSHIP SKILLS

To make a relationship work, you not only need the right partner but you also need to be strong in your relationship skills. Once you have attracted your mate, how will you two continually co-create? By assessing what does and doesn't work in your relationships, you can practice creating even better relationship skills in all areas of your life, starting today.

Exercise:
Your Strengths and Weaknesses in Relationship Skills

In your dating journal, use the following categories to rate your current levels of relationship satisfaction on a scale of 0 to 10, with 0 being the least satisfying and 10 being the most satisfying. If you are not currently dating, rate yourself based on your past dating relationships. What areas need improvement?

Trust =
Boundaries =
Communication =
Support =
Friendship =
Sexuality =
Honesty =
Intimacy =
Other =

Next, examine the areas that need work and create an action plan to address them. For example:

Honesty = 6 ⟶ *I will practice this relationship skill by speaking truthfully to friends about something difficult twice this week.*

Look at each category and create one action step to raise it one point this week; practice honing your skills with the people you interact with on a daily basis. The refined skills you will gain are the foundation of any healthy relationship, and they will translate to a great relationship with your partner when the right one comes around.

You have now learned to see the best in yourself and others, to create a clear and positive message about what you want, and to assess what you will sacrifice and gain by having the relationship of your dreams. You have even taken responsibility for brushing up on your relationship skills. Now, more than ever before, you are ready to start looking for your ideal mate!

10

SEE CLEARLY: SIZING UP A NEW RELATIONSHIP

With your newfound skills for actively pursuing a relationship and meeting people, you can now practice conscious dating. In this chapter we'll explore concrete ways to date. These new tools will help you stay true to what you want in a partner so that you do not fall into your old Dating Trap and will help you look closely at what is real between you and your date. After you have gathered your information, you can see if your date is really acceptable. But do not think you will change your date. The only job you have is to see who your date is and decide if you can live with it.

While you're doing the following exercises and check-lists, please keep in mind that this is dating and not the Spanish Inquisition. The people you date are human—

wonderful and imperfect. You are not looking for a perfect person because that person does not exist! You are looking for someone who is great for you. So, use these tools as a way to explore your feelings and reactions, and avoid getting sidetracked by powerful emotions and judgments. Use them to date consciously.

Top Five First Date Dos and Don'ts

DO have fun and look for the positive.

DO remind yourself of what is great about you.

DO try to learn something from every date.

DO be true to your values and standards.

DO be willing to be surprised.

DON'T replay all your past relationships.

DON'T discuss marriage and plan your future.

DON'T judge and criticize your date.

DON'T lie about who you really are.

DON'T blame yourself if it isn't a match!

Exercise:
Your Dating Checklist

After your dates, glance through the following questions and note your observations in your dating journal. You will be surprised how much you can already know on date #1. Using the blanks, add any of the items that were on your non-negotiable list from the last chapter and anything else you deem important.

- Is he nice to the waitress?
- Is he punctual? Reliable?
- Does he listen and show interest in you?
- How does he treat his friends?
- What is his family like?
- Does he take care of himself?
- How does he characterize his past relationships?
- Does he discuss his feelings and communicate?
- Does he know what is important to him?
- Do you have fun together?
- Do his actions match his words? Is he honest?
- Can you be yourself with him?
- Is he supportive of you?
- Is he independent?
- What does he want from a relationship?
- _____
- _____
- _____
- _____
- _____
- _____
- _____
- _____

It's easy to be blinded by love, the excitement of a first date, and the giddiness of a new experience. Asking yourself these questions right from the start will help you clarify important issues before you get carried away.

EXERCISE: RELATIONSHIP-WORTHY CHECKLIST

In your dating journal, jot down what you notice about your date in each of these important areas:

1. Fun
2. Consideration
3. Values
4. Interests
5. Acceptance level
6. Family
7. Friends
8. Respect
9. Mutuality
10. Communication
11. Responsibility
12. Chemistry
13. Romance
14. Generosity
15. Honesty
16. Self-care
17. Self-esteem
18. Commitment
19. Openness/intimacy
20. Impulse control
21. Health
22. Financial health

23. Relationship vision
24. Spirituality
25. Other

YOUR INTERVIEWING FORM

Learning to interview your dates is very important. Imagine that you were a CEO and hired a general manager because he was cute and made you laugh! A potential life mate is a very high-level position in your life. You want to make sure there is a reasonable match between who that person is and what you need them to be. No one will be perfect but they can be close enough to be workable. In interviewing you create a partner description (like a job description) to develop units of conversation and see if they can lead you to co-create your vision.

For example, Shana went on a date with an attractive man who was two years younger than her. She wanted marriage and children in the next two years and communicated this. He replied, "Oh, I won't be thinking of that for at least five years." Shana was disappointed but she knew that he had done her a favor. Before becoming emotionally invested, she could decide that a family was very important to her and the right man would support this. It was a good thing that she brought it up instead of trying to hide it.

Many women hide what is important to them for fear of displeasing their date or rocking a perfectly pleasant dream boat. The problem is that reality will eventually hit, and it won't be pretty. The best way to see who is a good match for you is to reveal who you are and see if he can accept and support it. This does not mean you have to agree on everything, but some parts of your relationship vision you will be unwilling to give up. In the interviewing process, you reveal what's important to you and when you see there is no match, you may choose to stop dating that person.

For example, Prana was a career woman who was passionate about her work. She knew that even if she had children, she wanted to continue working. She also knew that she needed a husband who was supportive of this. Many of her friends told her that successful, ambitious women were a turnoff to men. They told her to downplay her ambition. Prana decided to do the opposite and to share her passion. She found that it was true that many men did not like it when she said she would always want to work, even as a mother. Then she found a man who loved her passion and talent. He made her feel she could do anything and he was more than willing to support her progress and dreams. In the end, revealing her true self brought her what she wanted and stood for.

Once you are thinking about becoming serious with a potential partner, it's time to find out if the things that are important to you are also important to this person. It does not matter whether you like different hobbies and colors, but if he wants a wife who doesn't work and your career is your passion, pay attention.

An interviewing form helps you determine three crucial things: whether your partner fits with your Life Vision, whether your partner has the seven most important things you want in a partner/relationship, and whether you can accept each other as is. If you need a reminder, look back in your dating journal for the exercise where you defined your most important values for a partner.

It is not only crucial to notice what a man says, but you must also notice how he says it and what action follows.

Dating Interviewing Tips

1. Know yourself.

2. Have a clear Life Vision.

3. Have key questions reflecting things that are most important to you.

4. Practice revealing those issues in conversation.

5. Learn to gauge people's reaction.

6. Based upon the response, determine if you match on those issues.

7. Ascertain how much you have in common.

8. See if the differences are workable.

9. If there is a key issue that is unworkable, move on. Next!

10. If there is enough in common, continue to share who you are over time.

Does he consider what you want? Is there clearly no fit? Does he bring it up again? How important is this to you? For example, if you say "I'd like to live on the beach and have two kids," and he says "I don't want children and I will live only in the city," you need to either reevaluate your desires or move on.

Exercise:
Your Interview Items

To do this exercise, take out your dating journal and create three columns titled "What I Want," "Ways to Share It," and "My Partner's Reaction." In the "What I Want" column, list your dreams and things that really matter to you, based on your Life Vision. Then, in the "Ways to Share It" column, write down some possible ways to broach the subject to your date. For example, if you've always wanted to spend half of each year working abroad, see a foreign film from the region you're interested in and then engage in a discussion about it. Record your date's reaction in the third column. Then ask yourself if his reaction is workable. Did anything bother you about it? Why? How might you explore the topic further? Remember that a good fit will stick around and try to meld your two visions. You may choose to compromise too, but not on the most important things.

Exercise:
Differences and Similarities

Another way to get a sense of whether you and the person you are dating have a shared life vision is to highlight your differences and similarities. No two people are going to share exactly the same vision. In the following chart, you are the left circle and your date is the right circle. Your circles are connected like the infinity symbol. Over time you will determine what you have in common (the shared space where these two circles overlap) and what the important differences are (the things in each individual circle). Depict this chart in your dating notebook, so you can see what your similarities and differences are over time.

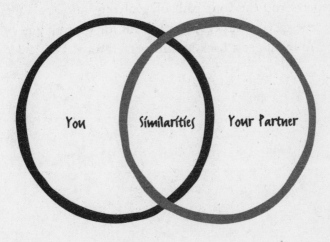

FIGURE 6: My Partner and Me

Determine whether you can communicate well about your differences now and how important they are. How you approach your differences can determine the success of a life-long relationship, so pay close attention to this area. (For more examples and suggested discussion techniques about working with your differences, you may wish to order my workbook *Shared Visions* by going to mydatingschool.com.) It will give you many questions to ask about, whether you can create a shared vision and take your relationship to the next level.

If you use this chapter's conscious dating tools and find the mate of your dreams, keep in mind that there is always growth work to do. I laugh when my clients say to me, "Everything will be easy once I meet my husband!" Marriage has its own learning process and requires openness and commitment. Having engaged in this dating process prepares you for your path of evolving intimacy. Vibrate the energy of love wherever it leads for yourself and others. You will get it back in unexpected ways.

11

Take Action Now: Transforming Insight into Action

You have arrived at the second-to-last chapter of this book with a wealth of new knowledge about yourself, your Life Vision, your best match, and dating tools for choosing the right partner. Now it's time to actively look! Most of us hate this part and would rather wait for The One to ring the bell. Take responsibility and make a commitment to act! I often ask new clients how much they want a relationship on a scale of 1 to 10 and they say 10. Then I ask them what action they've taken in the last month in the dating realm. Invariably they look down sheepishly and give themselves a 2 for action; usually they went out twice to a bar. They can immediately see the disconnect between what they say they want and the action they have taken to get it. How would you rate yourself this month for your dating action? In this section we will create a great dating résumé for you so that you will have a strong list of specific ways to meet people and you will walk your talk.

We'll also look at many practical dating considerations, such as dating during different life stages, how to steer clear of jerks, how soon to have sex, and how to handle differences in religion and spirituality. We'll end this chapter with answers to some frequently asked questions. Let's get started!

Exercise:
Dating Action Plan

This exercise will help you decide what actions you will consistently take to meet that special someone and create the relationship that you have been formulating in your mind's eye. This is an essential part of my sessions with clients because having a concrete plan is one of the greatest indicators of success. Without a plan, you can easily revert back to simply wishing about a relationship. It's time to put all the work and self-reflection you've accomplished into practice!

To begin, list all your ideas for action to take in your dating journal. Then assign dates on your calendar to make sure that you follow through. Here is a sample list:

- Online dating
- Fix-ups/Blind dates
- Classes
- Classified ads
- Clubs

Ten Ways to Create
Your Dating Action Plan

1. Be clear about what you want.

2. Make a comprehensive list of dating actions.

3. Choose up to two dating actions you will take each week.

4. Mark those events on your calendar.

5. Decide if you will go alone or with a friend.

6. No excuses—be accountable.

7. Praise yourself for your commitment, regardless of the outcome.

8. Journal about the lessons received.

9. Ascertain whether that location is worth a return visit.

10. Keep the faith and choose two events for next week!

- Bars
- Charity Events.
- Conferences & expos
- Parties
- Other

Modern dating has given singles a fabulous tool: online dating sites. There's a wide world of singles and possible connections at your fingertips if you just take the first step. If you haven't done so already, I strongly suggest including Internet dating into your dating plan. We'll talk about this in more detail in the next chapter.

How Do You Get To Carnegie Hall? Practice, Practice, Practice!

Once you have your dating plan, set a goal for yourself of going on at least one date a week, and apply all that you have learned:

- Be yourself.
- Know your Life and Relationship Vision.
- Know your strengths.
- Know what you have learned from past relationships.
- Know your relationship essentials and deal breakers.
- Have a positive Dating Context.
- Proceed with self-acceptance.

Anything in life requires practice, including relationships. Take time to date and learn about who you are and how you behave in your relationships. We all think dating is about meeting the perfect mate. It's really about becoming the partner that you want to attract. Take a look at the seven things you want in a partner, and apply diligence toward being those things yourself. Take time to practice this everywhere in your life so that you are ready when the right person comes along.

SEVEN TELLTALE SIGNS TO SPOT A JERK

It is also wise to be prepared when the wrong person comes around. If you spend any amount of time dating, you're bound to encounter a jerk or two. Take Miriam's story. She tried online dating and loved acting, so she looked for men with similar interests. One man asked her to meet him for a drink across town. She agreed, and rushed to meet him after a long day at work. They sat down for drinks and he proceeded to show her his whole acting portfolio and regaled her with his accomplishments for two hours. He asked nothing about her, not even if she wanted another drink. After he was done, he asked her, "So, do you think I'm a good actor?" Dumbfounded, she responded by saying, "Well, you certainly seem passionate about it but I've never seen you act, so how could I really know?" He shot her a look of fury, got up, and left without a word. He didn't even pay the check.

To help you better spot a jerk, be on the lookout for these seven characteristics:

1. *They only care about themselves:* These people care only about their own interests and agenda. A jerk doesn't care if you want to see a movie. If he wants to watch the game, then you're watching the game. There are many variations on this theme.

2. *They don't keep their word:* A jerk will say that he will come to your birthday party and then show up at the last minute. This is a recipe for heartbreak. If this is a pattern, run.

3. *They don't care about your feelings:* This is a man who will watch his favorite comedy while you are crying about your best friend's accident. When you need support and comfort, this jerk is absent.

4. *They have low self-esteem:* These people don't feel good about themselves and they act this out in different ways, all of which hurt you. For example, a man with low self-esteem might show off in sports and ignore you. He might insult you because you said something constructive and it triggers his own self-loathing. Rather than trying to heal a person who really doesn't like himself, recognize it and move on.

5. *They treat others badly:* A lot can be learned by how people treat their friends, their family, and, often most tellingly, strangers. He may be really gallant with you, but notice how rude he is to the waitress or how he curses at his mother. His true self is revealed in how he treats everyone, not just you. So pay attention.

6. *They only hear what they want to hear:* This is the kind of person who won't take no for an answer. He tries to persuade you to have sex when you're not interested. He may consistently ignore you when you request something important, like for him to lower his voice when a baby is sleeping. He is unable to accept that he may not always be right and that sometimes he may have to adjust his expectations and compromise.

7. *They lie:* This is the kind of person who will do all kinds of slimy things, from cheating on tests, to making up a fake excuse to cancel your date when something better comes along, to two-timing you. He may be attractive and charming but you can't trust him and you will never know where you stand. If you feel like you can't make heads or tails of the situation, it's probably because he is a liar. How can you know what's real if he is not?

Exercise: Jerk Alert

To familiarize yourself with jerks so you can steer clear of them, use this exercise to record your interactions with jerks. Describe some jerky dates and record the signs that signaled you and how long it took you to figure it out. By the end of the first date? Months? Or maybe even years? Take some time to reflect on how you'll tell sooner next time. Remember to keep your sense of humor. Hopefully you at least got a free drink.

SPECIAL DATING CONCERN: SPIRITUALITY, SEXUALITY, AND DIFFERENT LIFE STAGES

Matters of Spirit

Daters often wonder how much they should reveal upfront about their faith or spirituality to potential partners. And my answer is that it depends upon the extent to which you prioritize your faith. An extremely religious person whose faith is central would want to address this right away. For that person, it would be disruptive to become too emotionally involved with a partner who had a very disparate lifestyle. For people whose faith is more relative, it's fine to leave it out. These daters may want to reveal themselves over time and discern how willing they are to compromise and embrace an evolving vision of what faith could look like in their relationship.

In your early interactions with a date, it's typical to share basic information such as hobbies, favorite places, and travel. Slowly partners share about increasingly important things. It is good to be honest from the start but also appropriate to share parts of yourself over time, allowing intimacy to gradually deepen. The reason for this is because there is a temptation to place a potential date in a "box" based on religious beliefs, nationality, political orientation, and so on. While these things are important, no one thing represents a person on a deep level. It is important to know and be known over time to get a complete experiential picture.

However, I have witnessed the downside of waiting too long to talk about religion when it is a deal breaker for you. I had a coaching client who came to me upon ending a good relationship of two years over this issue. He was Jewish and she was Christian. Neither had wanted to rock the boat by bringing up this issue. She always figured that they would both compromise and create a joint experience of faith. He assumed that she would convert to Judaism if they married. When the relationship reached the level of engagement, religious differences became a deal breaker and they ended the relationship. The real underlying issue was one of no open communication, not respecting the importance of faith for each one of them and the inability to create a shared vision they could both accept. I am not suggesting that he should have compromised his faith; I am saying that if he was clear sooner and had communicated his position, it would have been better for them both.

In my opinion, the best time to discuss religious beliefs and practices is briefly in the beginning (to discern extreme definite positions) and then again in greater depth a few months after becoming exclusive. The reason for this is that for as long as you can date other people, you are not losing anything by spending time with someone, even if it doesn't work out. Once you close the door on other dating possibilities, though, your job is to see if there is a good fit long-term. This determination includes examining issues like spirituality, money, children, and values. Perhaps most importantly, spirituality is just one platform for observing the level of mutual respect, compromise and authentic communication between partners. There will be many challenges and what counts is whether you can find a mutually satisfying way to face them together.

If you and your partner don't share the same spiritual or religious beliefs, that doesn't mean that there is no hope for your relationship. It is up to the two of you to explore the best way to handle it if the other person does not synch up with your beliefs is to choose how that will affect your life going forward. If you are not planning to have children and just want a companion, perhaps this discrepancy would affect your daily life, values, and priorities very little. If you intend to marry and raise children together in a certain faith, you need to look at how you and your partner are willing to compromise and whether you can embrace compromise down the road. Say, for example, that you are atheist and your partner is Christian. Are you willing to attend religious functions, Christmas dinners, and so on with your partner and his family? After taking an honest look, if you are not happy with this choice long-term, end the relationship and be honest. Let them know they are a wonderful person and you wish the circumstances were different. Explain that upon introspection you cannot in good faith embrace a future that is not aligned with your true self.

"Should I or Shouldn't I?": When to Consummate the Relationship

Another common dating dilemma is when is the right time to become intimate. My client Carrie was divorced, with a twenty-two-year-old son, and had met a number of younger men who were attracted to her. They all said that she was brilliant, beautiful, and classy but didn't call back after the first date. She wondered if it was because she didn't jump into bed with them on the first date, which was something she considered inappropriate. She wondered when the right time was to be intimate and if she should adjust her ideas of appropriateness. Her ideas about sex were formed during her conservative Catholic upbringing, where the subjects of money and sex were considered "dirty."

My first piece of advice to Carrie was that she needed to figure out what sex meant to her. It does not matter what it meant to her parents, her religion, the men she dates, her snoopy neighbors, or her best friend. The answer to this question requires that she ignore the other influences in her life and be straight with herself.

Look at what voices drown yours out

Ask yourself what forces motivate your choices regarding sex? Here are some common pressures:

- Upbringing: Your parents may have told you that sex should happen only within marriage.
- Religion: Various religions often teach that sex is something to be ashamed of and that it is just for procreation.
- Dates: In the past, a date may have made you feel guilty for not "putting out" after an expensive dinner, or may have expressed frustration with not getting further physically after going out for a while.
- Peers: If your friends are getting a lot of action, you may think you should be too.
- The media: People on TV sleep together on the first date, giving us viewers the impression that something is wrong with us when we feel differently about it.
- Low self-esteem: Women often worry that men won't continue to date them if they don't have sex. Or some women become accustomed to thinking of sex as a bargaining chip; by withholding it, they think they will gain more interest and create challenge in men's minds.

The above outside forces can pull you in many directions and cause guilt and doubt. If you can reason with these influences yourself, great. If these forces continue to be powerful, you may consider going to therapy to address your guilt from the past that is getting in the way of your ability to be present. In the end, stay true to yourself. If you are living a life aligned with your beliefs, the right person will stick around. Yes, if that involves waiting longer to be intimate, he may complain, but if he respects who you are then he will decide that waiting is worth it. Likewise, if you choose to have sex on the first date, the right partner won't judge you but will stay around to get to know you in other ways. Make this choice upon introspection and discussion with your partner. Do not do it while you are horizontal! Take the focus off your dates and the outside world and choose what makes sense to you. Recognize that your feelings about intimacy can change as you grow and experience more.

Exercise:
Tune In to Yourself

In your journal, describe your values regarding sex. Ignore the messages you get from television, magazines, your friends, and your upbringing. What does it mean to you now? What would you need to know about your relationship before sleeping with a date? For you, how long does this normally take? What would you say to your date to let him know how you feel and what you need regarding sex? Write about it in your journal so you are clear going forward.

Exercise:
How to Know When It's Time

Sex means different things to different people. Some women have sex for fun and don't assume any level of attachment; others need to know that he will call the next day; some women need a level of friendship; others need to be in a committed relationship; and some women are saving themselves for marriage. There is no general "right or wrong" regarding when to have sex with a new partner, but it requires knowing yourself.

You may find it helpful to imagine different situations regarding intimacy and gauge your reaction. Whether you're about to go out on a first date or you've been seeing someone for some time already, reflect on the following questions:

- How would you feel if you had sex, you had a great time, and then he never called again?
- What if he called you and continued to sleep with you—and others?
- What if you didn't have sex and just kept the relationship more platonic?
- What if you were both monogamous but he never wanted to marry?

Think of other questions to ask yourself. Let your mind wander over different scenarios to get a better sense of your feelings. Be straight with yourself about what sex means to you practically, emotionally, and spiritually from the beginning and take responsibility for it. Then speak your standards if you need to. Have a conversation to see what you both expect. Do not make him wrong if he has another opinion. It's his right. Just choose to stand by your belief. Don't keep quiet about your expectations and then blame your partner for having a different agenda. Although sex might mean marriage to you, it may just be fun for him! If you did not discuss it then you did not consciously create what you wanted.

If you decide to hold off on having sex while dating, it is important to let your date know that you care about him in other ways. You can express that you care for him verbally or through hugging, handholding, or kissing. You can make him dinner or send him a card. Everyone wants to be appreciated, so let your date know your standards are about you and not about him. Remind him how special he is and how much you enjoy his company. Listen to him and ask what is important to him. Appreciate who he is and support him. This is as valuable as sex. Also, straight communication about why you are choosing to postpone sex avoids unintended pain and rejection on both sides.

Dating at Different Life Stages
People come to the dating scene from all kinds of life stages and circumstances. And everyone has a shot at finding the right person. Let's look at some of those stages now.

Dating after divorce
Dating after divorce can be difficult because you are going back into the fire. You believed in love and your vows and were very disappointed. You may even have a husband who cheated on you and may now feel like you can't trust men. You thought you were through with dating forever. How can you create something different now?

I know it's not easy. In part 1 of this book you unloaded past baggage, limiting beliefs, and looked closely at what you have learned and what you want to create going forward. When you feel bitter, afraid, and stuck, a therapist can help. It is important that you work through and release the pain before creating a new lifetime relationship. Remember the Law of Attraction: what you vibrate, you attract. So, you need to create a positive outlook before you date. Get clear about what you now deserve to create and what you can offer and receive in a relationship. Step into a powerful vision and remind yourself every day of what you are going to attract and why you deserve it.

Midlife dating

At midlife, you may feel like you've missed the boat and have no idea how to date. You're not alone, you're just rusty! I had a client who came in for coaching and did not use email or know how to "google" local dating events. He did not enjoy bars and preferred concerts and classes as venues to meet people. We tailored his action plan to his personal needs and he had more success. You, too, can tailor your dating plan to work for you.

Be encouraged. According to AARP 30 percent of the nation's 77 million boomers are single and 70 percent of these are regularly dating. And 45 to 48 percent are having sex more than once a week. In fact, AARP now has a relationships section you can find at aarpmagazine.com. They have message boards, personal ads, and a "modern love" column. So unlike popular belief, love opportunities for seniors are plentiful. It is never too late to start again, and you can do it in your own way and in your own time.

Today people are living very long, full lives. Why live it alone? There are mature dating sites like 50yearsplus.com

Top Reasons Why Dating Only Gets Better in Midlife

1. You know yourself and what you want.

2. You appreciate every moment.

3. You really don't care about what others think.

4. No need to worry about becoming preggers!

5. You have more free time and money.

6. You have strong self-esteem.

7. You are clear on your priorities.

8. You've always wanted to be "Mrs. Robinson"!

and singles activities, classes and groups to meet like-minded people in your age range.

Many universities now have interesting divisions for seniors where you can socialize and learn. A great example is NYU's Osher Lifelong Learning Institute or OLLI (scps.nyu.edu/learning). Here mature adults who are scholars and practitioners lead workshops, classes, and panels drawing on their expertise. Share your wisdom and meet interesting people. See if your local universities offer something similar near you.

Do not ignore your need for companionship and affection. You have earned the right to focus on you now and have some fun! So, if you have a single friend to go to events with, go! If you need extended support, hire a dating coach or write to me for some beginning advice. Do not give up on yourself or on love. The best is yet to come.

Dating as a single parent

Dating as a single parent can be difficult because parenting is your second full-time job and you are doing it alone. Also, some single parents worry about having a prospective date because they assume childcare burdens early on. Another fear is about having your children become attached to prospective dates who may be transient. All of these are things to work through, but they are not reasons to forgo love and partnership! There are dating sites and organizations like Parents Without Partners that lend support, guidance, and the opportunity to meet others in the same situation. You can also get a dating coach to help you marshal your resources and date successfully.

A question that I frequently get from single parents is when to share that you have a child. It is good to do so early on (between the first and third date) because it is something important and unalterable about you. The right partner will value your commitment to being a good parent and will be open to the possibility of being one too.

FREQUENTLY ASKED QUESTIONS

Here are some frequently asked questions. I'd love to hear your questions too. Feel free to email them to me at kpaulet@verizon.net.

Q: Who pays on the first date and afterward?
A: This is a question that each person must answer individually. It is commonly thought that if a man asks you out that he should pay on the first date. I tend to agree but it really depends on the situation, the two people involved and their finances, their philosophies regarding dating, equality, chivalry, and so on. You also need to be clear about who you are dating and that person's lifestyle. For example, a teacher or social worker may have a strict budget. They might love to spend time with you but can't afford to go to fancy restaurants or travel regularly unless you go dutch. It is up to you to decide if you can accept this financial situation or come to another solution. There are plenty of ways to make your date feel special that don't involve money.

Take a look at the reasons that you set limits around a date's financial situation. Many of my female clients start out telling me that they only want to date someone who makes $400,000 and up. When I explore why, they say it is what is expected of them or that looks successful. Examine whether your beliefs about finances come from a conscious choice about your values and preferred lifestyle or if they derive from the expectations of others. Otherwise you may forgo a very sweet, sensitive, supportive mate in favor of a wad of cash. These soul-searching questions should be answered before you seriously date. This issue is particularly confusing to women today because many are successful in their own right and don't need to be taken care of by a man. Whatever your choice, be clear. What often tears marriages apart is when a woman marries a low income provider expecting him to change. When he doesn't, she makes them both pay for the rest of their lives. And there is not enough money in the world worth that!

Q: What are signs that my date is serious about the relationship?

A: When a relationship is moving forward, there are some telltale signs. Your date will consistently want to call and see you. You will be a priority in his life, as evidenced by him integrating you into his family, friends, and important events. He may also begin to include you in conversations about the future, hinting at living together and more. There are also signs that a date is not serious:

- He usually does not call when he says he will.
- He is in and out of your life and relationship.
- He refuses to discuss marriage, the future, or commitment.
- He has broken off other engagements and is a commitment phobic.
- You have been dating three-plus years and there are no signs of increasing intimacy or change.
- He continues to date other people after a year.
- He does not include you with family, friends, or important celebrations, after a year of dating.

Q: What constitutes dating versus "friends with benefits" or a fling?

A: My definition of dating is a romantic relationship with the potential for a long-term commitment or marriage. A fling is often short-term, with an unlikely possibility of a long-term relationship.

I often get asked, "If a male friend sleeps over a lot, are we dating?" The sarcastic "traditional" answer is, "Only if he buys you dinner." But seriously, one of my major points is that there are no rules. What matters is the intentions and heart of both people. The only way to clarify that is to discuss what your relationship means to both of you and where it is going. Do not assume anything. What matters are your mutual expectations, intentions, and needs regarding exclusivity, commitment, and long-term goals.

Q: Are there different reasons for dating?

A: Yes. People do date with many intentions. An "unready" man or woman will date for fun, excitement, romance, sexual gratification, experience, to learn about the opposite sex, or to learn about themselves. These are all good valid reasons for that person to date.

Some people date to establish a long-term meaningful relationship and partnership, while others date to marry and establish a family.

Trouble enters when we assume that our dates have the same intentions as we! Online profiles are good because there is often a section where you click your intention, such as "dating for fun," "dating for long-term relationship," or "seeking marriage." If this isn't clear, you need to bring it up early on in your relationship. There are instances where an unready man who is "just having fun" does find himself in love and ready for greater commitment, but you cannot count on this. So, be an informed conscious dater and choose to wisely invest your time with open eyes. Since we attract who we are, you will usually remain in relationships with partners who are at the same level of readiness as you.

Q: When should I become exclusive?

A: I find that many people want a relationship so much that they meet a nice, attractive partner and commit to them by the second date. Some of this is sex driven, because they feel they need exclusivity to become intimate. Another reason is they are desperate to snag a partner and make their dream come true immediately! I had a prospective coaching client who said to me, "I want to commit to someone in a few dates and get married in six months!" This was in the realm of possibility but I questioned, "Can you even know who you are committing to for a lifetime in that amount of time?" She answered, "No, but at least I can say I am married!" Then she said that half of marriages end in divorce and 30 percent of married folk are unhappy. And we wonder why! We need to look at why we are getting married. Are we marrying the milestone or the person? I worked with her to raise her self-esteem and enjoy her life so she could only welcome appropriate matches into her life.

If you are a prize, do not settle and jump into exclusivity before you know the person you are committing to. It's desperate and won't lead to a good outcome. It rules out other possibilities. Know what you are looking for and be an observer to see if you are in the ballpark with your prospective partner. This can take at least four months of due diligence. Then if you become exclusive it is your job to interview the person and see if he is the one you want to marry. If you find something does not fit and cannot be worked through you need to end the relationship and begin dating again. Do not stay long-term because it is comfortable—you will waste valuable time.

Q: I've been dating for a while and still haven't found the right person. Should I get back together with my ex?

A: Sometimes we go through negative experiences to help us learn what we want. Recall why you broke up with your ex. Was he controlling? Maybe at the time you learned that you want someone who embraces you as is. Be clear what you want to attract so you do not get the same results as before. Many people look at a former relationship and wonder if it was a mistake to end it, especially if they haven't found anything that compares. Often there are good reasons that you broke up in the first place. Many times partners who get back together find themselves right back where they started.

One client of mine, Sandy, was forty years old and wanted a baby. She had loved Patrick in college but they were on again, off again and he never treated her right. They stayed long-distance pals over the years. After his divorce, he was lonely. She shared her dream of having a child and he suggested they try again. She visited him with the hope of conceiving. When she arrived they began to argue and continued to annoy each other. By the second day she was ready to fly home. She could not tolerate him, despite her great desire to have a child.

Sometimes people separate for reasons of age or circumstance, not because of their relationship issues. For example, there are people who date in high school, marry other people and divorce, and find each other again. Another factor is emotional timing. For example, Andrea dated her boyfriend for two years and then moved in with him; with the understanding that they would get engaged. When the time came, Tim got scared. He refused to tell her when he would be ready to take this step. Andrea said that she wanted marriage and if they were not on the same page, she would leave. A month later, Tim proposed to her and said that he did not want to live without her. When two people reunite in clarity and love rather than fear, outcomes are better.

Here is my advice for anyone considering getting back together with an ex:

- Do not return to the relationship expecting that the other person has changed.
- Check if you are just remembering the good, out of sentimentality.
- Be clear about the reasons you split in the first place.
- Be realistic about the ways that the relationship will be different.
- Act out of love and clarity, not fear and loneliness.
- Ask yourself if there was a lesson to be learned the first time. Did you learn it?

Q: I have an interesting but demanding corporate position and come home exhausted and drained most nights. How am I supposed to meet someone?
A: It is not always easy to balance what we value in life but it is important to try. For you, work is already going well

but you want to manifest a romantic partner now. Your actions need to match you words. See what you can do to delegate at work and set boundaries. Then figure out when you can commit to going out and meeting people. It is very important to put in the effort even if it means beginning slowly by allotting one weekend day to this area of your life and then building upon that. Take baby steps and see how opportunities open up.

Q: I am a woman interested in a man. Is it ever okay to make the first move?

A: This is another dating rule I'd love to bust. I think it's okay to make the first move sometimes. You can send a wink online or say hello at the coffee shop. Why not ... you are just being friendly.

In a survey by match.com, 87 percent of women said they had considered making the first romantic move if attracted to someone and 27 percent of married women had contacted their future husband via email on a dating site. An estimated two hundred thousand members met their mate on dating sites in 2003.

I am not saying to chase men. You are a great catch and the right person will know it. But this is 2008 and you are a powerful creator! Don't let anyone tell you otherwise. If you want to initiate contact, go ahead and take a risk for love.

12

INTERNET DATING: YOU'VE GOT MAIL

If you are unfamiliar with new dating methods, this chapter will serve as a quick review of Internet dating. Internet dating has made it easy to meet someone from the comfort of your own home. According to a recent report from Nielsen, the marketing research company, one in three internet users have used the web to meet a partner. It's no wonder, as the internet offers many dating advantages. For one thing, it reaches into many geographical locations. You can access a dating site twenty-four hours a day and the monthly cost is usually cheaper and more convenient than going to many singles events. And you can operate on your own schedule and communicate via email and phone until you are ready to meet in person; all you need is a computer.

If you don't have much experience with computers, the Internet, or email, don't let fear of the unfamiliar stop you from using this resource. Rest assured, you CAN learn! So while it's beyond the scope of this book to get into greater detail, I will tell you that you can find a friend or even pay someone to teach you. And there are often computers available for use at your local library or copy shop.

After you familiarize yourself with the Internet and get settled with an available computer, here are some simple steps to help you start online dating:

1. BROWSE THE INTERNET FOR DATING SITES

Check out the sites I list below to get you started. There are sites to suits all kinds of personalities and interests. Today there are dating sites for every preference: religious affiliation, spirituality, pet lovers, vegetarians, college grads— you name it. Some popular, general sites I recommend include jdate.com, match.com, and eharmony.com. Dating sites often charge a membership fee of between $30 and $40 per month. If this sounds steep, I've also noted some free dating sites with an asterisk.

50yearsplus.com (over 50 years old)
agematch.com (intergenerational singles)
animalattraction.com (pet owners)
Bisexualpassions.com (bisexuals)
bbwromance.com (big beautiful singles)

bookloversonlinedating.com* (singles who love to read)

chemistry.com

conscioussingles.com (spirituality)

conservativematch.com (politically conservative singles)

craigslist.org*

dateagolfer.com (golfers)

datemypet.com

deafsinglesconnection.com (deaf singles)

democraticsingles.com (politically progressive singles)

divorcedpeoplemeet.com (divorced singles)

docdates.com (people with all kinds of doctorates and masters degrees)

eharmony.com

fitkiss.com (fitness and sport singles)

friendfinder.com*

gayfriendfinder.com (gay men)

gk2gk.com (smart geeky singles)

gothicmatch.com (gothic singles)

greenfriends.com (vegetarians and animal rights activists)

interracialcupid.com (interracial singles)

jdate.com (Jewish singles)

largefriends.com (plus-size singles)

lavalife.com

lovebyrd.com (disabled singles)

match.com

megafriends.com*

militaryfriends.com (singles in the service)

myspace.com*

pairings.us (singles with a passion for food and cooking)

plentyoffish.com*

rightstuffdating.com (singles from top tier universities)

shypassions.com (shy singles and introverts)

singlebooklovers.com (singles who love books)

singleparentsmingle.com (single parents)

singleparentlove.com (single parents)

soberandsingle.com (sober singles)

tall.org (tall singles)

thesquare.com (select colleges)

thirdage.com (mature singles)

trekpassions.com (sci-fi fans)

true.com

vddate.com (singles with STDs)

veggiedate.com (vegetarians)

2. CREATE YOUR PROFILE

Often this means taking up to five simple steps.

PICTURE:

A. Get a digital picture of yourself to post on your profile. Using your own or a borrowed digital camera, take a picture of yourself (or have a friend do it for you), download the picture onto a computer, and then upload your picture by following directions on the site. If you only have a regular, printed snapshot, you can take it to a local drug store or camera/photography store and have it put on a disk. From there, you download the image onto your computer as a "jpeg" file and then upload to the site. A picture is very important because it makes it eight times more likely that you will receive a response from a potential date. If all this "downloading, uploading" talk makes your head spin, ask a computer-savvy friend to help you.

ESSAY:

B. Many sites require short essays about who you are. Review the exercises where you wrote about your strengths, accomplishments, and Life Vision. Draw on these descriptions to write a positive description that truly represents who you are.

PARTNER:

C. Some sites require essays about the type of relationship and partner you want. Review the exercise you did in chapter 9 describing the seven qualities you want in a mate and what you won't accept. You can write it in a positive, nonjudgmental way. Revisit your Relationship Vision and your list of what you would gain from a relationship. Integrate this information to write about what you want in a relationship and mate.

INTERESTS:

D. Many sites ask you to describe your interests. Review your "Date Yourself Record" from chapter 7 to remember the types of things that you enjoy doing in your free time.

REVIEW:

E. Make sure that you are clear about the profile you are sending out. Remember, you attract who you are, so you want to present an accurate and powerful picture of your vision. This will save you time in the long run and will help you avoid mismatched dates.

BE CONSISTENT:

F. Online dating is a time commitment. Be prepared to spend a fair amount of time browsing profiles of potential dates and responding to people who are interested in you. I have many friends and clients who overwhelmingly agree that it is time well spent.

3. MEET IN PERSON

Many daters wonder when to move from email to an in-person meeting once they've been corresponding with a person for a while. Should they meet as soon as possible or keep on emailing? My answer is that there are advantages to both approaches:

Five Advantages of Meeting Immediately:

1. You can only gauge chemistry in person.
2. Meeting in person eliminates some potential for misconceptions and lies.
3. You don't spend as much time in fantasy.
4. You date in "real time" and share experiences beyond the computer.
5. You start to integrate into each other's lives.

Five Advantages to a Long Emailing Period:

1. You get to know someone's inner self first, before seeing the outside.
2. Corresponding can be intimate and gives you the opportunity to learn things about the other person.
3. It feels safer to get to know someone with some built-in distance first.
4. You can slow things down and prolong the courtship.

5. It can increase mystery, romance, and desire.

Overall I advise people to exchange emails for up to a month and then meet. To be on the safe side, I recommend meeting in a public place and not disclosing your home or work information. Nothing compares to a face-to-face meeting when it comes to getting to know a person.

HOW TO DEAL WITH ONLINE DECEPTION

When you meet someone over the Internet, there's always the chance that the person is not who he says he is. It is common these days to exaggerate your qualities while dating in order to gain acceptance. Up to 33 percent of internet users admit to lying to some degree on their online profiles. Men usually lie about their height and age and women lie about their weight and age. Some daters misrepresent their age, physique, income, marital status, spirituality, location, parenthood, and dating intentions just to impress a potential mate. Popular dating books even suggest faking who you are in order to seem more attractive and mysterious. They suggest that you adopt rules of conduct completely different from your own, so the other person does not even know who they are dating!

People who encounter this type of deception come away with the impression that people online are liars, that online dating simply doesn't work, or even that people in general are not to be trusted. It is incredibly disappointing when you think you were getting to know someone, and that person was not being authentic.

Ethical or not, daters often subscribe to societal norms and expert rules as the best approach. Many just want to be loved and feel that who they really are is not good enough. This will make you angry because you feel that you've wasted your time. It is also no way to build a foundation based upon trust, honesty, and authenticity.

It is hard for people to communicate their true selves. But it is only by being yourself that you can possibly learn who is right for you. You may be surprised. For example, a divorced man with three kids (that he is tempted to deny) could be the perfect match for an older date who cannot have her own children. Sometimes what makes you unique is the exact thing that the right person will find especially intriguing and loveable.

As for how to deal with others' deception, remember not to fall too hard before you meet your date in person. So much is revealed when you take your relationship into real time. Most importantly, don't lose faith. You can't control other people but you can be the example. The more honest people are on the Internet, the better for us. So be proud of everything you are and share it. You will meet a person who responds in kind and is delighted by your honesty. It is the inner change of one person at a time that affects dating as a whole. If everyone was honest and accepting, what a different experience the dating world would be.

Starting something new is often overwhelming, and online dating is no different. Break it down and take one step a day. If it still feels unfamiliar, ask a friend who is good with technology to help you. When you need an energy boost, confide in a friend who can keep you on track. The important thing is to get started!

13

DATING RESOURCE GUIDE: INSPIRING RECOMMENDATIONS

You have come a long way and will continue learning on your dating journey. In this chapter, I offer my list of resources to keep you informed and inspired along the way. Feel free to add your favorites or recommendations from friends so you have a wide selection to choose from any time you need a new dating idea.

BOOKS

Ask and It Is Given by Esther & Jerry Hicks (Hay House, Inc., 2004). A thorough exploration of the principles of the Law of Attraction and ways to use it.

Conversations with God by Neale Donald Walsch (G.P. Putnam's Sons, 1996). Solid guidance on how to access your higher self and develop your capacity to be love in this world.

The Dark Side of the Light Chasers by Debbie Ford (Riverhead Books, 1998). A great book for learning to recognize and defuse your triggers in your relationships.

Date . . . or Soul Mate? by Neil Clark Warren (Thomas Nelson Publishers, 2002). Gives tips to help you decide if someone is worth pursuing in two dates or less.

Dateworthy: Get the Relationship You Want by Dennie Hughes (Rodale Press, 2004). A fun, hip advice book for women looking for love.

Gift from the Sea by Anne Morrow Lindbergh (Pantheon Books, 1955). A beautiful book about the gift of solitude and the process of learning about yourself.

Simple Abundance by Sarah Ban Breathnach (Warner Books, 1995). A great book to help you appreciate your life and take good care of yourself.

This Time I Dance! by Tama J. Kieves (Jeremy P. Tracher/Penguin, 2003). A story about trusting your inner voice on an unknown journey and letting what fits reveal itself.

Wishcraft by Barbara Sher with Annie Gottlieb (Ballantine Books, 2003). An inspiring book on finding new ways to create your dream life.

INSPIRING MOVIES/SHOWS

Because I Said So (2007). A young woman's mother tries to fix her up, and they both learn a lot in the process.

Bridget Jones's Diary (2001) and *Bridget Jones: The Edge of Reason* (2004). This single heroine looks for true love and discovers it in an unexpected package.

Broken English (2007). A single woman dates and experiences many disappointments, until she finally finds love.

Hitch (2005). A dating coach teaches men tricks to attract women and learns that it was them being their true selves that did the trick.

How to Lose a Guy in 10 Days (2003). A single magazine writer experiments with a dating story and learns something about herself, and love, in the process.

Knocked Up (2007). A young woman becomes pregnant and finds herself with someone very different than her usual "type." They learn to love each other in unexpected ways.

Legally Blonde (2001). A young woman learns to trust herself and becomes more discriminating about whom she wants as a partner.

Miss Potter (2006). A writer follows her dream and her own ideals about love. By being her true self she is led to meet her life partners, both of whom love and support her vision.

Must Love Dogs (2005). A middle-aged woman tries dating online and meets her love.

Never Been Kissed (1999). A young woman returns to dating with high hopes and little experience.

The Perfect Man (2005). A middle-aged single woman finds herself settling for the wrong men. As her self-acceptance grows, she meets the right mate.

Picture Perfect (1997). Our heroine dates to impress others and schemes and lies about who she is. Over time she reveals her true self to others and realizes in the process that she has found real love.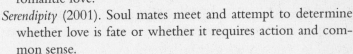

Sense and Sensibility (1995). Though the experiences of two sisters, we see the difference between idealistic and mature romantic love.

Serendipity (2001). Soul mates meet and attempt to determine whether love is fate or whether it requires action and common sense.

Sex and the City (1998). Four single girlfriends explore dating in NYC and share their lessons.

Shallow Hal (2001). A young man learns that love is more than skin deep.

Under the Tuscan Sun (2003). A woman left by her cheating husband sets out to create her own life and to discover love along the way.

When Harry Met Sally... (1989). Two single friends redefine the nature of their relationship over time and find a profound love they had overlooked.

Working Girl (1988). A woman begins to trust herself and to create her own life. She learns to be discriminating about the type of partner who will support her goals and treat her well.

You've Got Mail (1998). A bookstore owner tries online dating and discovers that sometimes your soul mate comes in a surprising package.

DATING COACHING SERVICES

I started My Dating School (mydatingschool.com) as a place where singles of all kinds could share dating issues and learn from their experiences in a supportive, inspiring environment. It is based in Manhattan but offers services and online community membership to people globally, including individual coaching by phone or email, teleclasses (classes by phone), and weekend retreats. Visit the site for more information.

THERAPY

In therapy the focus is usually on the past, helping you to clear past events and limiting beliefs so that you can take action in a new way. It is important to choose a therapist who is a good match. The best way to find a therapist is by recommendation from someone you respect. If that is not a viable option, consult your insurance company or psychologist directories such as psychology today.com. Once you meet a therapist, interview him or her to see if there is a good match for your needs and personality. For more detailed information about what to think about when choosing a therapist read the article at healingwell.com/library/health/grold1.asp.

To find a dating coach, the best way is personal referral. If someone had a good experience and made some progress with that coach than you may want to check him or her out. You can also tell something about a coach's philosophy by reading their book or hearing them present at a workshop. If these suggestions are not possible, go to a directory such as coachfederation.org and read the coaches' descriptions there. These coaches have finished an accredited coaching program but they may not specialize in dating and might not have an additional academic background or degree in counseling or psychology. So, be clear what questions you want to ask them before you set up your first meeting and always use your best judgment.

FUN ACTIVITIES AND CLASSES

There is a large variety of classes and activities where you can meet new people. To name a few: wine tastings, athletic activities, museum openings, library events, readings at book stores, the gym, singles cruises and vacations, walking tours, musical venues of all sorts, book and movie clubs, volunteer activities, political organizations, marches and rallies, environmental groups, religious community gatherings, the local YMCA, cooking classes, adventure outings, dance classes, dances, clubs, bars, online dating sites, matchmakers, hobby and special interest classes, and civic/community meetings in your area. The point is to get out and see what inspires you! And don't forget that the Internet is the perfect resource for finding opportunities like these.

SINGLES EVENTS

Get on the Internet and use a search engine like Google (google.com) to locate singles events in your area. You can also look at the newspaper or ask other singles where they go. Initiating this conversation can be a good way to invite a new single friend to go to an event with you. Use your dating journal to keep a list of single friends you can take to these events and friends, family, and coworkers who can fix you up. Don't be shy!

TOP TWENTY-FIVE CITIES FOR SINGLES

For your next vacation, consider checking out one of the following destinations, which have the highest percentages of singles in the nation. I even know people who have relocated in order to be in a wider dating pool!

Rank	City	% population single
1	Bloomington, IN	58.2%
2	New Brunswick, NJ	54.6%
3	College Station, TX	54.3%

4	Ames, IA	52.5%
5	Iowa City, IA	52.0%
6	Cambridge, MA	52.0%
7	Somerville, MA	51.3%
8	Boston, MA	50.4%
9	Berkeley, CA	50.3%
10	Champaign, IL	50.2%
11	Davis, CA	49.6%
12	Gainesville, FL	48.7%
13	Boulder, CO	48.4%
14	Washington, DC	48.4%
15	Ann Arbor, MI	48.4%
16	Tallahassee, FL	48.2%
17	Athens-Clarke County, GA	48.1%
18	Greenville, NC	47.6%
19	Lawrence, KS	47.1%
20	Jacksonville, NC	46.9%
21	Camden, NJ	46.6%
22	Minneapolis, MN	45.8%
23	Syracuse, NY	45.6%
24	Kalamazoo, MI	45.5%
25	Santa Cruz, CA	45.3%

HIGHEST PERCENTAGES BY GENDER

Most **male** singles:
1. Los Angeles, CA
2. Phoenix, AZ
3. Las Vegas, NV
4. San Francisco, CA
5. Seattle, WA

Most **female** singles:
1. New York, NY
2. Boston, MA
3. Philadelphia, PA
4. Washington, DC
5. Miami, FL

BEST CITIES FOR QUALITY OF LIFE FOR SINGLES

1. Baltimore, MD
2. Austin, TX
3. Atlanta, GA
4. Boston, MA

5. Los Angeles, CA
6. Phoenix, AZ
7. New York, NY
8. San Francisco, CA

Explore your own city as if you were a single tourist. What advantages does it have that you have overlooked? This will provide more opportunities to meet people while having fun.

TAKING STOCK

It is important to consolidate what you have learned on this *Dating from the Inside Out* journey. On a note card, fill out the following sentences. Keep this card in your wallet and review as needed.

My Dating Vision

The past hurt that kept me trapped was:

My old Dating Context / unconscious want ad was:

My underlying desires / conscious want ad is:

So my new Dating Context / Dating Action Plan is:

The relationship I will create will be:

I am now committed to:

AFTERWORD

Being single and dating may be a challenging chapter in your life because the process is full of uncertainty and rejection. Most people feel that dating is worth it because they believe in the amazing satisfaction that comes from having a loving, exciting, giving relationship—one of the most incredible joys in life. I hope this book has shown you that dating does not just have to be a means to that end. Dating can also be a way to gain clarity about who you are and what you want in your life. It can also be an opportunity to meet different people and have new experiences that lead you to become a better person and a better partner.

In life there are many ups and downs, layoffs and promotions. When you marry yourself despite these rollercoaster circumstances, you are better prepared to approach your relationships the same way. The dating journey then helps you to accept and love yourself so you can better allow others to really love and know you. Maintaining this positive Dating Context, creating dating opportunities, and taking risks to reveal yourself will attract the right mate for you. Remember to be humble and kind; many people have been hurt when it comes to love, and some daters take their time before they commit and fully trust. Remember too, that if it is right, the ideal person will stay forever. The important part is not to give up on yourself in the process. Create a readiness on the inside and results will follow.

I wish you peace, learning, and joy on your dating journey. Let me know what happens!

My best in life and love,

Paulette Kauffman Sherman

Paulette
kpaulet@verizon.net

> *Visit my website mydatingschool.com to learn about services, my online community, and to sign up for my free monthly newsletter.*

GLOSSARY

Accomplishments—things that you've done that you and others are proud of

Action Plan—a plan that specifies actions you will take in order to get to a specified goal

Commitment—to pledge something or someone

Conscious Dating Journal—a book in which to write what happens on your dates, in order to promote awareness and making good choices regarding that person.

Conscious dating—dating while awake to what is really going on

Conscious Want Ad—a composite of the type of partner you really want to choose

Dating Action Plan—a plan consisting of specific action steps you will take in order to meet your life mate

Dating Baggage—painful old beliefs, feelings and experiences that we still carry with us that prevent us from moving forward in our relationships in a new way

Dating Calling Card—a card that describes what is amazing and distinctive about you

Dating Context—the space you have to create a new relationship depends upon your interpretation of your past dating experiences, beliefs, and feelings

Dating Fatalist—someone who thinks that love happens without action or will

Dating Gremlin—the negative voice that tells you disempowering things about dating

Dating from the Inside-Out—looking within yourself to create your ideal relationship before expecting it to just happen outside

Dating Interviewing—asking pertinent questions to see if a prospective date meets the most essential requirements of the type of partner you most want

Dating Karma—the effects of all deeds create past, present, and future experiences, making one responsible for one's own life

Dating Myths—popular stories about dating, believed to be false

Dating Trap—the particular negative dating situation that you repeat

Dealbreakers—things you will not accept in a partner or relationship

Defensive Dating Style(s)—a dating typology of defensive styles, representing different ways that singles protect themselves in romantic love

Defensive Dating Style—an unconscious strategy used to protect yourself from getting hurt, in the context of romantic love

Essentials—the most important things you want in a partner and relationship